THOUGHTS

of

WISDOM

The Simple Truths

JOHN C. NEWMAN

WESTBOW
PRESS®
A DIVISION OF THOMAS NELSON
& ZONDERVAN

WestBow Press books may be ordered through booksellers or by contacting:

WestBow Press
A Division of Thomas Nelson & Zondervan
1663 Liberty Drive
Bloomington, IN 47403
www.westbowpress.com
844-714-3454

ISBN: 979-8-3850-2727-9 (sc)
ISBN: 979-8-3850-2728-6 (hc)
ISBN: 979-8-3850-2729-3 (e)

Library of Congress Control Number: 2024912001

Print information available on the last page.

WestBow Press rev. date: 09/09/2024

CONTENTS

CONTENTS

DEDICATION

To my family and friends.

Special Thanks

To the heavenly Father through Whom all blessings flow.

In remembrance:

My profoundest gratitude is reserved for my great-grandmother, mom's father's mother, "Grannie." I recall her tireless patience and the precious wisdom she shared, as well as her warm, loving embrace and calm demeanor. She valiantly endured the persecutions of slavery, and I'm certain she continues to watch over the family and awaits our heavenly arrivals.

I fondly recall my mom's parents, "Granddaddy" and "Grandma," granddaddy's brother, my grand uncle, and my mom's sisters, my aunties. Mom's elder sister and her husband both passed away long before I was born. I have memories of stories shared that paint a vivid picture of a beautiful, stately, loving lady and her husband, my uncle, a brave patriot who served his country with distinction in WWII, as did my father. As life would have it, my eldest sister, younger sister, and two younger brothers all served in the Armed Forces with distinction, as did I.

I was often told stories about my dad's parents: his mom, "Ma-Minnie," of whom I had a great fondness, and his father, "Daddy-Richard," who passed long before my birth. I was told he was a man with unique foresight and astuteness, a stern, caring, and gentle soul.

My fond memories also include my dad's mother's siblings, my grand uncle and grand aunt, as well as his siblings, my uncles and aunts. My existence was shaped by the magnanimity and synergy of their lineage.

To my late mother and father: Without them, there would never have been "Thoughts of Wisdom {The Simple Truths}." Their love, spirit of loyalty, and self-sacrifice inspired me to always endeavor to become more than I was. They instilled in me a life philosophy, a learnedness of integrity and honor, and the significance of sharing and caring for family, friends, and others.

To my late father and mother-in-law: for their love, caring, sharing, and guidance.

To my strongest supporters: my beloved wife of over 42 years, giving me her adoration and unwavering support; my wonderful son, who can be rebellious at times, reflecting back at me the pure genuineness only youthful passion can give. Together, they have enriched my life beyond my wildest dreams. To my late elder brother, a loving soul who passed away much too early. To my elder and younger sisters, my younger brothers, my wife's younger brother, and to my plethora of beloved cousins and myriad of nephews and nieces who taught me fairness, balance, and justice, which became a way of life that continues to energize me today.

To my lifelong friends, whom I will not attempt to name for fear of omitting someone precious and dear. You are aware of your significance and how deeply I treasure your friendships. Without your caring, non-judgmental attitudes, and loving understanding, it would have been extremely challenging to keep my focus.

To my extended military family, for which there are no words to describe the forever revered bond.

Blessings and heartfelt thanks to each of you.

1

ELDERS' COUNSEL

In life, the wisdom and guidance of our elders are invaluable. As the middle child among seven siblings, I learned to appreciate these pearls of wisdom early on. When my great-grandmother, grandmother, and grandfather spoke, even my parents paid attention. Thus, whenever I craved extra treats or sought solace, I turned to my grandparents. My memories of them are cherished and dear.

Embrace this concept, as it will serve you well. Save your money, and your money will save you.

—DAD, MR. R. NEWMAN

You know that you're only saying those nice things about me because they're true!

—MOM, MRS. A. NEWMAN

Don't talk a lot—listen; you will learn more. Your education is very important.

—AUNT, MRS. B. KIMBRELL

Even though kids grow up into adults, our job of parenting is never-ending.

—DAD, MR. R. NEWMAN

When asked something my mother-in-law didn't know, her response was, "I must tell you that I haven't got a clue!"

—MOTHER-IN-LAW, MRS. H. DUVNJAK

Family is the most important part of life. Do whatever you can to ensure they are taken care of, but don't let them bring you down.

—DAD, MR. R. NEWMAN

Don't ever get it in your head that you're smarter than everybody else. That's not nice.

—Grandmother, Mrs. M. Newman

Nothing will be more valuable to you than having good schooling.

—Granduncle, Mr. L. Monroe

You need to work hard to make something of yourself. It won't be easy.

—Uncle, Mr. S. Jenkins

"Let me see," said the blind man, and still he couldn't see a lick!

—Dad, Mr. R. Newman

To get ahead in life, you will need to get yourself a good education.

—Mom, Mrs. A. Newman

Anytime you want to make the good Lord laugh, just let Him know what you think is going to happen!

—Grandmother, Mrs. M. Smith

Use sugar and honey when you deal with people, and you won't need a lot of salt and pepper.

—Grandmother, Mrs. M. Newman

When asked, "What do you think will happen next?" My father would respond, "We shall see what we shall see."

—Dad, Mr. R. Newman

When we are approaching the end of our lives, it matters not who we are. In our final hours, we are all left with the same thing—our memories.

—Dad, Mr. R. Newman

Don't ever put having a good time in front of your schooling.

—Grandmother, Mrs. M. Smith

In many situations in life, the desired outcomes are sometimes a far cry from what you wanted to happen. This is what's called a lesson in reality.

—Dad, Mr. R. Newman

I know you're all grown up, and you don't want me telling you what to do. I just need you to know I'm telling you anyway.

—Mom, Mrs. A. Newman

My good man, an honest trade is no swindle.

—Dad, Mr. R. Newman

Actions taken out of necessity are governed by no known laws.

—Dad, Mr. R. Newman

Don't let the devil show you the way to a good whipping!

—Great-grandmother, Mrs. R. Smith

You need to stay away from jealousy and vanity. They are good friends with the devil.

—Great-grandmother, Mrs. R. Smith

Don't think that just because everybody has a head on their shoulders, it means they have common sense in it.

—Grandmother, Mrs. M. Newman

Just because you didn't get caught today doesn't mean I won't catch you tomorrow!

—Grandfather, Mr. J. A. Smith

Put your mind to it, and you can be anything that you want to be.

—Grandmother, Mrs. M. Newman

You need to understand that hard work never hurts anyone. It will help you.

—Uncle, Mr. W. Bush

Take your time and do it right the first time, and you will go far in life.

—Grandfather, Mr. R. Newman

If a task wasn't yet completed, my father-in-law's answer would always be, "It's a big, big job. I need a little more time."

—Father-in-law, Mr. M. Duvnjak

If you scratch a lie, you will find a thief.

—Unknown author
(*Honor and integrity are not embraced by all.*)

Children ask parents excitedly, "How will Santa Claus get from the roof and into the house to bring us our toys? We don't have a chimney for him to come down!" The parents answer with a smile, "Don't worry. He'll climb down, knock on the front door, and Mom and I will let him in. But Santa won't come until you go to bed and fall asleep."

—Mom and Dad, Mrs. A. and Mr. R. Newman

Tell me the truth. What really happened? There is always a possibility that you can avoid the spanking. But the punishment, my good man, look forward to it.

—Dad, Mr. R. Newman

My John-John was dressed so sharply that every time he moved, he cut himself!

—Aunt, Mrs. N. Williams

I know what you said you wanted for Christmas, but Auntie knows what you need.

—Aunt, Mrs. N. Bush

Having a good education is immeasurable; those who have one will fare well in life.

—Dad, Mr. R. Newman

Any time you want to go fishing, ask me. If it's a good day, I'll take you.

—Grandaunt, Mrs. I. Davis

You need to understand that if you can bet on it, it can be fixed. And it usually is.

—Uncle, Mr. O. Newman

It doesn't matter what the circumstances are. What matters is that you do the very best you can.

—Uncle, Mr. T. Williams

Don't let Mr. Bad and Miss Wrong get you in trouble.

—Great-grandmother, Mrs. R. Smith

If it is to be done, then it is to be done. So, let it be done quickly.

—Dad, Mr. R. Newman

You need to decide what you want to be and do everything you can to make it happen.

—Aunt, Mrs. M. Jenkins

Thoughts of Wisdom

Don't ever step over a dime to pick up a nickel.

—DAD, MR. R. NEWMAN

Families will have disagreements and sometimes altercations. Always be aware that family is God-sent. Love them.

—MOM, MRS. A. NEWMAN

Don't you let anything get in the way of your schooling.

—GRANDMOTHER, MRS. M. SMITH

Our four-year-old son asked us, "Why are people different colors and sizes?" We responded, "That's the way God wanted them to be."

—SON, MR. J. NEWMAN II; MRS. AND MRS. J. AND D. NEWMAN

A ninety-eight-year-old gentleman was asked a few days prior to his upcoming birthday, "What would you like to do on this auspicious occasion?" His answer was, "Be there to celebrate it."

—VENERABLE SENIOR GENTLEMAN

If you really want to help yourself, get a good education.

—UNCLE, MR. T. WILLIAMS

When mundane tasks become difficult, you will have reached the golden years of life.

—DAD, MR. R. NEWMAN

Don't ever overlook the importance of your education.

—Aunt, Mrs. A. Gaines

The only way you'll get old is to live long enough.

—Dad, Mr. R. Newman

Come over here and give me a hug and a kiss. It doesn't matter how old you are; you'll always be my baby.

—Mom, Mrs. A. Newman

Life is what you make of it. Do what you need to do and stay in school.

—Uncle, Mr. L. Newman

You will need a good education if you're going to make it in the world.

—Aunt, Mrs. N. Williams

Stop pouting. When you grow up, you will see how smart your mother and father are.

—Grandmothers, Mrs. M. Newman and Mrs. M. Smith

There is nothing in the world more precious than family. No matter what they do or say, you have to love and forgive them.

—Grandmothers, Mrs. M. Newman and Mrs. M. Smith

You will minimize your regrets in life if you always do your best.
—Cousin, Mrs. R. A. Ivy

I know. I'm so sweet, the honeybees are going to take me away!
—Mom, Mrs. A. Newman

Get a good education. It will never fail you.
—Aunt and Uncle, Mrs. M. and Mr. B. Bassie

Understand that your friends and who you hang around with reflect on you. So do the best you can to make sure they're good people.
—Grandmothers, Mrs. M. Newman and Mrs. M. Smith

Fret not, for all is well that ends well.
—Dad, Mr. R. Newman

If you treat everybody nice, the good Lord will smile at you.
—Great-grandmother, Mrs. R. Smith

You better stop crying, or I will give you something to cry for.
—All of the elders at some time or another

It's essential that you always be truthful with yourself, no matter how painful it may be.
—Dad, Mr. R. Newman

You need to understand me. Trouble and no good will always follow a liar.

—GRANDMOTHER, MRS. M. SMITH

The world you are growing up in is far more treacherous than it was for your mom and me. However, it's also more supportive and rewarding. If you prepare yourself to meet the challenges and take full advantage of the opportunities, you will fare well in life.

—DAD, MR. R. NEWMAN

Our adult son informed us, "Understand these are modern times. There is a new way of thinking. Dad, you and Mom are old school." We responded, "What's important for you to discern about old school is that if and when batteries die, electricity goes out, or the internet goes down, we will continue to function. You, your calculator, cell phone, Google, Siri, and Alexa can't."

—SON, MR. J. NEWMAN II; PARENTS, MR. AND MRS. J. AND D. NEWMAN

2

LIFE LESSONS

Humanity will always cherish and uphold the teachings from life's lessons. Wisdom is passed down through generations, a process that requires precious time. Our patience and readiness to learn are essential for absorbing the lessons of life.

When I was young, I wanted to stay that way. Now that I'm old, I am delighted it didn't happen. I see how much of life I would have missed if I had.

—John C. Newman

You are not inferior. Feeling inferior requires your consent. Don't ever give it up.

—John C. Newman

Choices in life will not always be easy. You will always have a choice, but be aware that many of the choices you make will not be correct. Have the courage to stand by them.

—John C. Newman

The only things we are entitled to in life are those we earn.

—John C. Newman

Focus on the positive aspects of life. The not-so-good things will inevitably reveal themselves.

—John C. Newman

Life is unique. Life is precious and, at times, unforgiving. Take advantage of every moment.

—John C. Newman

Life is life. The challenge is that we try to make it what it's not. Utopia is only in our dreams.

—John C. Newman

In life, all we can do is give our best. The universe determines the final outcome.

—John C. Newman

There is no such thing as perfection. Life is comprised of all kinds of people and riddled with liars and thieves. Our only recourse is to choose between the lesser of the evils.

—John C. Newman

Anxiety makes us pause, and imagination gives us hope. Our willingness to act is what matters.

—John C. Newman

Individuals unwilling to work in life will receive from life what a blind person sees.

—John C. Newman

Our minds are the most precious and powerful things in the world. It is tragic how so many of today's youth are wasting theirs and giving no regard to the consequences.

—John C. Newman

A crucial lesson in life is learning when to leave our egos at the door.
—JOHN C. NEWMAN

What makes life so amazing is that occasionally just showing up is sufficient.
—UNKNOWN AUTHOR (*THE UNIVERSE IS ALWAYS AT WORK.*)

We must be mindful of the fact that no matter how much we desire those around us to succeed in life, we can only control our own destiny.
—JOHN C. NEWMAN

Life is not fair. This is not a perfect world. Countless things will happen that are not to our liking. Stay committed, get over it, and move on.
—JOHN C. NEWMAN

Sometimes there is a major disparity between what we can do and what we assume we can do. We must be cognizant of the fact that the latter is what gets us into a dilemma.
—JOHN C. NEWMAN

Nothing has value until value is given. It is imperative that the value we place on things be valid, for when we give unwarranted value, we give away our integrity.
—JOHN C. NEWMAN

Sometimes life gives us a myriad of choices. So, when and if it does, we must take our time and choose wisely.

—John C. Newman

It is not always about winning; it should always be about having a winning spirit.

—John C. Newman

Each day, say to yourself, "I'm going to have a fantastic day!" If you don't, let it be a surprise, not a foregone conclusion. That's true positive thinking.

—John and Danelia Newman

There is nothing wrong with being greedy if you aren't wasteful. To have and not need is to be prudent.

—John C. Newman

There are two proven strategies to live a life of total financial freedom: be blessed with wealthy parents or get off your lazy butt, work hard, and make it happen!

—John C. Newman

Do not waste time thinking about how not to make the same mistakes twice. The wise thing to do is to concentrate on not making new ones.

—John C. Newman

There are only two ways of doing things: the right way and the wrong way. There is no other way. Your way doesn't count.

—John C. Newman

Your home may be your greatest financial asset, but the biggest financial investment is your retirement and maintaining an exceptional quality of life.

—John C. Newman

When I became a young man, my parents told me to go out into the world and seek my fortune. That's what I did. It enriched my development and education.

—John C. Newman

We do not choose our lives, and the time we have to live it is Godsent.

—John C. Newman

Our children are a lot like us: smart, confident, passionate, stubborn, and opinionated. At times, they make us angry. That is the time to remember that they did not ask to be here.

—John C. Newman

Our children are the best of us. They are also the worst of us. The splendor of life is that they are blessed with being themselves.

—John C. Newman

The difference between a villain and a hero: A villain is hated while a hero is loved, or perhaps the difference simply depends on our vantage point!

—JOHN C. NEWMAN

When friends or family members share with you that you have a striking resemblance to your parents or relatives, the response should be, "You're right, and that's how it should be."

—JOHN C. NEWMAN

Common sense is not common. In fact, it is the least common intellect of all.

—JOHN C. NEWMAN

Those who have not raised children of their own cannot truly comprehend how complex a task parenting is.

—JOHN C. NEWMAN

It is self-defeating to make decisions when you're enraged. Your thoughts radiate reprisal, your mind is cloudy, and your actions challenge logic.

—UNKNOWN AUTHOR *(THIS IS THE TIME TO BE PRUDENT.)*

Life's design is for us to live in the present. Life can be short, and time is fortune.

—JOHN C. NEWMAN

If you are looking for a panacea to the challenges of life, stop. It does not exist; you are wasting precious time.

—JOHN C. NEWMAN

Live each day like there will be no tomorrow. Today has been so graciously given to us, and tomorrow is not a foregone conclusion.

—JOHN C. NEWMAN

Yesterday is gone forever, and tomorrow is not promised. Today is where our focus must be. Life can be brief; time is a bonus.

—JOHN C. NEWMAN

Life can and will be wonderful and pleasurable if we focus and give it the opportunity.

—JOHN C. NEWMAN

No one will ever be able to predict the future. If that day should ever arise, only a select few would be left here to enjoy it.

—JOHN C. NEWMAN

To those among us who have not yet experienced the magical persona of Déjà Vu, you have this delightful experience to look forward to.

—JOHN C. NEWMAN

It is not vital to agree with or get along with everyone, but it should be compulsory that we be civil to everyone.

—JOHN C. NEWMAN

Whoever started the adage that a dog is man's best friend was never attacked by a Pit Bull, Great Dane, Doberman Pincher, Rottweiler, or German Shepherd.

—JOHN C. NEWMAN

If today was a particularly good day, our goal should be to strive for a much better tomorrow.

—JOHN C. NEWMAN

As a young man, I thought money was one of the most important things in life. Now that I am in my golden years, I am certain it is. Some of life's most valuable teachings are learned early.

—JOHN C. NEWMAN

Love, happiness, right and wrong, bad, good, evil, joy, and pain. That's life!

—JOHN C. NEWMAN

It behooves us all to wake up and smell the coffee. It is definitely brewing!

—JOHN C. NEWMAN

What we frequently think about has a major influence on what comes about in our lives. Positive thinking should be a constant mindset.

—JOHN C. NEWMAN

If you would like to do nothing all day, you need to start early in the morning.

—UNKNOWN AUTHOR (*WAKING UP IS A BLESSING*).

If you decide to put off until tomorrow what you can do today, be certain you do it.

—JOHN C. NEWMAN

Everyone has an opinion, and those opinions will vary. This prerogative is invaluable when communicating.

—JOHN C. NEWMAN

The challenge with our youth today is that they are spending entirely too much time trying to find themselves.

—JOHN C. NEWMAN

We cannot take anything at face value. It is crucial that we check and re-check any information being disseminated. Trust and reliability are becoming ideas of the past.

—JOHN C. NEWMAN

Be careful how you choose friends or where you place your confidence. In today's world, mayhem is prevalent, and very little is what it seems.

—JOHN C. NEWMAN

Life will be constantly challenging. Just keep living it one day at a time and count your blessings.

—John C. Newman

We are all humans, not superheroes, no matter what we think or are being told.

—John C. Newman

Friendship, like trust, can only be earned. Once you have them, they are permanent and cannot be lost or taken; they are only pushed away.

—John C. Newman

Living your life as a generous giver and an excellent receiver personifies the true meaning of sharing and caring.

—John C. Newman

Most things in our lives are relatively simple until we make them complicated.

—John C. Newman

Eating too much chocolate is a mistake. Driving while intoxicated is a bad decision. Be mindful that the results of the latter are catastrophic.

—John C. Newman

In life, those individuals who focus on the bad, undesirable, and ugly usually find them.

—JOHN C. NEWMAN

Hospitals and prisons are two undesirable places. In life's journey, the first might be unavoidable; the latter should be avoided at all costs.

—JOHN C. NEWMAN

We should be civil to our neighbors, but their trust must be earned.

—JOHN C. NEWMAN

In life, money cannot buy everything, and everything cannot be replaced.

—JOHN C. NEWMAN

When I was a young man, I told myself that I would never get old. Now that I'm old, I realize how little about life I knew at the time.

—JOHN C. NEWMAN

We are all pupils enrolled in the World University, learning at our own pace.

—JOHN C. NEWMAN

We can have someone do our work, but it is impossible for someone to do our workouts.

—JOHN C. NEWMAN

Insanity personified is knowing something is going to happen, being warned that it is going to happen, and not taking any action to stop it from happening.

—John C. Newman

A brief, simplistic description of life: arriving, growing, changing, and departing.

—John C. Newman

The outcome of a game, even though we are on opposing teams, is no reason to not have enjoyed playing the game or remain friends.

—John C. Newman

Destiny is not a matter of chance; the web was woven long before we arrived. We make choices along the way; however, God has a purpose for us all.

—John C. Newman

We have lost sight of what it is and become obsessed with what we want it to be.

—John C. Newman

What transpires in our lives may not be decided by us. What we do in life is our choice, and we should always be accountable for it.

—John C. Newman

Thoughts of Wisdom

Become a steward of sharing and caring. The universe will repay your kindness by enriching your life.

—John C. Newman

To know how and not to do something is a waste of knowledge. Have the courage to act.

—John C. Newman

Attitude is the most important ingredient in the formula for creating changes in your life. Having the nerve to act makes change happen.

—John C. Newman

To live life without having loved and truly being loved is likened to never having seen or smelled the ocean, marveled at a rainbow, or felt the blissful touch of raindrops on your face. To miss these precious delights would be heartbreaking.

—John C. Newman

Negotiations are an invaluable part of life. We must understand and master the art of negotiation. In life, nearly everything is negotiable.

—John C. Newman

It is crucial that we be mindful of the power of words. It's not just what we say that makes us effective communicators. How we say things and the words we use create the distinction.

—John C. Newman

Computers, the internet, social networks, and smart phones. Learning technology is necessary in order to be able to function now and in the future.

—John C. Newman

We had nothing to do with how some of the most significant individuals in our lives came into our lives. Embrace their presence.

—John C. Newman

Family is everything. Love them unconditionally. When they pass on, it is too late.

—John C. Newman

It only takes a minute to think before doing something foolish that will take the rest of your life to recover from. Take your time and make informed decisions.

—John C. Newman

You are not perfect by any means. No one is. If you are not aware of this by now, I suggest you ask somebody—anybody!

—John C. Newman

There are numerous individuals who say life is too short, and from where they are sitting, that just might be true. The optimum word is sitting.

—John C. Newman

Commit to living life to the fullest, and how short it may be will not matter.

—John C. Newman

If, for some reason, you think you are the only one who cares, you are wrong.

—John C. Newman

Show me a person who does not believe in God or some form of higher power, and I'll show you a person who is on their way to the unpleasant alternative.

—John C. Newman

Life is fickle. It can make or break us, but it also gives us the tools we need to succeed and reconstruct. It is our choice if we use them or not.

—John C. Newman

Accept the truth about yourself, and your life will become more meaningful and simplistic. The truth is that you are only human.

—John C. Newman

Take more time to listen. You will be surprised by what you hear.

—John C. Newman

Treat every day of your life like a new beginning, because that's exactly what it is.

—John C. Newman

Staying on course in the face of uncertainty is affirming that you have courage and integrity.

—John C. Newman

Challenges and situations are going to happen in our lives. It always matters what happens; however, what counts the most is what we do when it occurs.

—John C. Newman

If you believe that you can make a positive difference in the lives of others, you can. And there is no better time to do so than the present.

—John C. Newman

What should I do with my life? The only person who can answer that question is you. So, stop asking and start doing.

—John C. Newman

In life, we must be mindful of the reality that there will always be a cost.

—John C. Newman

The younger generation spends much too much time thinking about being popular and how they look. What really matters is where they are going and how they get there.

—JOHN C. NEWMAN

Life is capricious, and occasionally we feel like it has given us a raw deal. When it does, our task is to create the means to cook it.

—JOHN C. NEWMAN

No matter how complicated the situation may get, if we trust in staying the course and taking decisive actions, common sense will nearly always prevail.

—JOHN C. NEWMAN

If you would like to reduce stress in your life, focus on things you can change. Leave things you cannot change to those who can.

—JOHN C. NEWMAN

If there should ever come a time in life when you feel you cannot go on, you can.

—JOHN C. NEWMAN

There will be times in life when the best course of action is to take none. Life is capable of taking care of itself.

—JOHN C. NEWMAN

A snapshot of life would be joy, pain, sunshine, and rain. That should cover it.

—John C. Newman

Life is too brief for us not to be frantically going after our wildest dreams.

—John C. Newman

The secret of life is time. Another secret is that no one knows how much they have.

—John C. Newman

What makes the game of life so wonderful is that it does not matter how talented we are. Everyone still gets to play the entire game.

—John C. Newman

It is written that the sick and the poor will always be with us. Those who control the wealth of the world will not have it any other way.

—John C. Newman

We are three different individuals: the person we are, the person we think we are, and the person everyone else sees.

—John C. Newman

Old soldier to young recruit: If I tell you a flea will pull a freight train, don't waste time asking how. You just find a way to hook him up!
—UNKNOWN AUTHOR *(FOCUS ON THE TASK.)*

Life can be likened to a complex jigsaw puzzle. It is extremely challenging to assemble, but we must continue to persevere. All the pieces are there.
—JOHN C. NEWMAN

Courage is something we all have—some of us more than others. It may be in diverse areas, and it may manifest itself at unique times. If we develop our character, courage will be there when we need it.
—JOHN C. NEWMAN

Sarcasm at its finest: "What time is it?" The answer is: "The same time it was yesterday, the day before, and the day before that." Must I go on?
—JOHN C. NEWMAN

It matters not what religion or faith we have; what matters is that we have one.
—JOHN C. NEWMAN

Affirmative action took more than two hundred years to institute. How ironic that we let the very institution that it was created to safeguard against tell us we don't need it, and we agreed with them.
—JOHN C. NEWMAN

If it weren't for some of those individuals we thought were fanatics doing wild and odd things, many of today's vital innovations would not have been discovered.

—UNKNOWN AUTHOR (*THIS IS WHAT MAKES LIFE AMAZING.*)

What in life would you be willing to give your life for? This is a critical question for anyone not to know. It is imperative that you find out and guard it with your life.

—JOHN C. NEWMAN

In the beginning and in the end, women will be women, and men will be men. There will always be those who are just not sure who they want to be. Love and embrace them.

—JOHN C. NEWMAN

Exercise boosts our energy and reduces stress. It also strengthens the parts of our body where we exercise the most. For quite a few people, it is their mouths.

—JOHN C. NEWMAN

No two children are alike. They are all endowed with God-given abilities. Parental leadership is essential. Trust that the positive instruction sticks, and they will make the correct choices in life. Those who do not, we leave in God's hands to shepherd.

—JOHN C. NEWMAN

Sometimes our friends are more loyal than our relatives. The dramatic irony is that we get to choose our friends.

—JOHN C. NEWMAN

Be aware that we will all make mistakes and errors. Take solace in knowing that life is just reminding us that we are human.

—JOHN C. NEWMAN

Do not stress over unfinished tasks. There is tomorrow, and even though tomorrow is not promised to anyone, those tasks will be completed whether we are there or not.

—JOHN C. NEWMAN

The grass is greener on the other side because we neglect to fertilize and water our own.

—JOHN C. NEWMAN

Looking back on our lives, it would be nice if we could be proud of it all and have no regrets. We must embrace the humbling realism of life. Perfection is out of our reach.

—JOHN C. NEWMAN

Throughout life's journey, we may not remember names or faces, but we will always recall how we were treated and by whom.

—JOHN C. NEWMAN

We will be presented with several ways tasks can be accomplished. There is only one way that matters, and that is the right way.

—John C. Newman

Live life with as little gray area as possible. Each day will pass with fewer challenges.

—John C. Newman

Time will tell how we will all be remembered. When we reach that juncture in life, the individuals being remembered will no longer have any, nor care.

—John C. Newman

The world is filled with honest and dishonest people. The task at hand is disseminating who is who.

—John C. Newman

Our ego controls most of us; our brain controls too few of us. Our mindset must change.

—John C. Newman

Facts are what matter; you can distort them as much as you please. What you want it to be will not change what it is.

—John C. Newman

Life determines who we are by what we do. Once we do it, it is done.
—JOHN C. NEWMAN

There is only right and wrong. Do not pursue a halfway compromise; it is not worth it.
—JOHN C. NEWMAN

When you have given your absolute best, there is no shame if it is not good enough.
—JOHN C. NEWMAN

No news is good news. But frequent updates would be appreciated.
—JOHN C. NEWMAN

Stating your case very loudly has no bearing at all on its validity. It shows ineptness.
—JOHN C. NEWMAN

Wishful thinking is wanting to have everything but not being willing to do anything.
—JOHN C. NEWMAN

Life has many faces. You should always be on the lookout for happy ones.
—JOHN C. NEWMAN

What a wonderful world we live in! We must do everything possible to keep it that way.

—JOHN C. NEWMAN

In life, when you get right down to it, we can only do the best we can.

—JOHN C. NEWMAN

Patience is a virtue we should all nurture. You will find it well worth the wait.

—JOHN C. NEWMAN

There is absolutely nothing you can do to replace your integrity and honor.

—JOHN C. NEWMAN

A smart person knows what to say. A wise person knows whether to say it or not.

—UNKNOWN AUTHOR
(*STRIVE TO BECOME BOTH.*)

More than wealth and fame, your goal should be to be the best person you can be.

—JOHN C. NEWMAN

Motivation and habits get you where you want to be. Make motivation a habit, and you will get there quickly. It is your choice.

—JOHN C. NEWMAN

The price we pay to gain knowledge is our commitment to ourselves to grow and develop our minds. What we receive in return is an enriched lifestyle.

—JOHN C. NEWMAN

Your attitude, positive thinking, and actions ultimately determine the quality of your life.

—JOHN C. NEWMAN

It is crucial that we get our priorities in life straight. Nothing will make sense until we do. So, decide what is important.

—JOHN C. NEWMAN

What life has to offer depends entirely on what you are willing to give and accept.

—JOHN C. NEWMAN

Having a viable plan is futile if you are not willing to act. So, move it!

—JOHN C. NEWMAN

We must learn to distinguish between the kinds of individuals who come into our lives. Some arrive to make positive change, and they will, but only if we allow them to.

—JOHN C. NEWMAN

Whatever you think you can do, why not try and do it? So, what do you think?

—JOHN C. NEWMAN

In life, when mistakes are made, there are lessons to be learned. When bad decisions are made, there is a price to be paid.

—JOHN C. NEWMAN

There are two significant facts we must understand regarding employment. Procuring the job is a job; keeping the job is the ultimate job.

—JOHN AND DANELIA NEWMAN

If you can imagine changing your world, you can! It is your choice to make.

—JOHN C. NEWMAN

The past teaches realism. We choose what to learn from it.

—JOHN C. NEWMAN

If you just lighten up, your days will amazingly brighten up.

—UNKNOWN AUTHOR (SO WILL YOUR LIFE.)

This world we live in can be unforgiving. However, forgiving is what we should be.

—JOHN C. NEWMAN

We are never completely out of control. You always have a choice. Take your time and choose wisely.

—JOHN C. NEWMAN

When we are young, we feel invincible. When we grow old, we feel our mortality.

—JOHN C. NEWMAN

Wishing, hoping, and dreaming without acting is a terrible waste of your time, and it places a tremendous burden on everyone else around you.

—JOHN C. NEWMAN

If society remains teachable, we will never stop learning and flourishing.

—JOHN C. NEWMAN

The power to choose is truly a blessing. Making informed decisions is crucial.

—JOHN C. NEWMAN

If you are experiencing challenges in your life and searching for something or someone to blame, stop wasting your time. Look in the mirror, and you will see the culprit.

—JOHN C. NEWMAN

Your integrity and honor are the most valuable gifts of all. They can never be taken; you can only give them away. Don't.

—JOHN C. NEWMAN

The past is there to ensure that we keep moving forward and have a future.

—JOHN C. NEWMAN

Learn to forgive yourself and your fellow man. You will grow and prosper in life.

—JOHN C. NEWMAN

In life, we should never let good enough be good enough. But giving our best effort is.

—JOHN C. NEWMAN

Keep things in your life simple. If it is right, do it; if it is wrong, do not.

—JOHN C. NEWMAN

Life will embrace us all when humanity realizes we must stop fighting amongst ourselves.

—JOHN C. NEWMAN

Commit to make changes in your life. Action will make the changes occur. Being true to yourself without compromise will change your way of life.

—JOHN AND DANELIA NEWMAN

Misery loves company.

—UNKNOWN AUTHOR
(*MISERY IS NOT A NICE COMPANION.*)

How we view the world is important, but not as crucial as how the world views us.

—JOHN C. NEWMAN

Trust is the most essential component in any relationship. Focus on building it.

—JOHN C. NEWMAN

Individuals who commit to do whatever it takes will always control those who do not.

—JOHN C. NEWMAN

Some people know how to live, and some people don't.

—KRISTINA LULIC
(*LEARNING HOW IS OUR CHOICE TO MAKE.*)

It saddens me to say that chivalry is not alive and well. In my humble opinion, it has been replaced by vanity, which is a trait of which humanity has more than enough.

—JOHN C. NEWMAN

It is imperative that you focus on living the life you have today, as your actions will profoundly affect your future.

—JOHN C. NEWMAN

We all want the absolute best in life for our families and friends. However, if this is to be realized, they must want it for themselves.

—JOHN C. NEWMAN

Confidence and curiosity are necessary to sustain optimal growth and development.

—JOHN C. NEWMAN

Old Chief to young Braves: Life is a struggle between two wolves, one good and the other evil. One brave asked the chief, "Which one wins?" He answered, "The one you feed."

—UNKNOWN AUTHOR
(*THE SAME APPLIES TO HUMILITY AND VANITY.*)

A lifelong friend is always there when needed. A fair-weather friend is self-explanatory.

—JOHN C. NEWMAN

In life, there will be different roads you can take to reach the same destination. The difference is the time it takes to get there. What matters is that we arrive safely.

—John C. Newman

The most challenging task in life's journey is enduring the passing of a loved one, family, and friends.

—John C. Newman

We must first understand what we are; only then can we understand who we are.

—John C. Newman

The reason for doing the right thing is because it is the right thing to do.

—John C. Newman

The past shows progression; the present shows actuality; and the future shows vision. Life encompasses them all. Stay focused and prepare yourself.

—John C. Newman

In life, there are those who do what is needed to have what they want and those who do nothing but what they are told and have only what they are given. You have a choice.

—John C. Newman

The circle of life is absolute and will not change. Embrace it! We are born, become youthful adults, grow old, and pass on. The fountain of youth is a fantasy. Do not be victimized by vanity and ego.

—JOHN C. NEWMAN

In life, the only certainty is its uncertainty.

—JOHN C. NEWMAN

Parenting is arguably the world's most demanding job. The absence of it is causing considerable distress among many of today's youth.

—JOHN AND DANELIA NEWMAN

We are all happy and get along fine right up until the time we choose sides.

—JOHN C. NEWMAN

Learn to live in the moment and keep an open mind. While we might not always agree completely, it is important that we continue to focus on the objective.

—JOHN C. NEWMAN

The reason for our existence is to search for our purpose in life and fulfill that purpose.

—JOHN C. NEWMAN

While having a conversation with our youth or any young person of this generation about where their life is going, if you receive a response such as, "I'm still trying to find myself," please help them with their challenge. Ask them to go look in the mirror.

—JOHN C. NEWMAN

Typically, it is not the suspects who cause us harm; more often, it is those we hold dear who betray.

—JOHN C. NEWMAN

Mistakes are intricate parts of life. What is crucial are the actions taken after making them. This is where our focus should be.

—JOHN C. NEWMAN

Each of us is special and unique. What determines our individualism is our attitude, integrity, honor, commitment, being teachable, and willingness to change our mindset.

—JOHN C. NEWMAN

What matters most in life is not where we started; it's where we end up.

—JOHN C. NEWMAN

Life's realism is simplified: there are those who can and those who cannot; those who do and those who do not; those who will and those who will not. What makes life unique is that all the choices are ours to make.

—John C. Newman

In life, those who dedicate themselves to preparation will greatly surpass the procrastinators.

—John C. Newman

Not being willing to accept the fact that sometimes we can be the challenge is a prime example of vanity and ego doing their drudgery.

—John C. Newman

One of life's amazing riddles is that there are two things we do not get to see coming, but we live them both: tomorrow and the future.

—John C. Newman

When we are young children, it is so easy for us to forgive and forget. When we grow into adults, it is not as easy to forgive, and we tend to forget.

—John C. Newman

Life has three universal treasures: love, joy, and happiness. Finding them will only take commitment, focus, and action. So why not achieve all three?

—John C. Newman

It is essential to recognize that nothing in life is truly new; we just found it out.

—John C. Newman

We must be willing to embrace the fact that what we want things to be and what they are will often be two vastly different things.

—John C. Newman

On the journey through life, there is no such thing as being on time. You are either early or late. If you arrive on time, something or someone has to wait.

—John C. Newman

These emotions in life should be avoided at all costs: vanity, envy, and jealousy.

—John C. Newman

Throughout our life journey, we will be tested and re-tested. Have the courage to stand tall in the face of adversity, and when needed, be humble, caring, and accountable.

—John C. Newman

In life, easy embraces the weak, and challenging seeks out the strong. What happens in our lives will be determined by the choices and decisions we make.

—John C. Newman

While dreaming is a wonderful part of our lives, the important thing is not to dream your life away.

—JOHN C. NEWMAN

We should pay close attention to young children at play. Their exuberance is what we lack as adults. The insight they have in the areas of interaction and harmony is invaluable.

—JOHN C. NEWMAN

When meeting life's challenges with forgiveness in your heart, integrity in one hand, and honor in the other, we will almost always be triumphant.

—JOHN C. NEWMAN

In the modern world, the focus isn't on right and wrong; it's on differing perspectives. Flawed reasoning and political correctness dominate. Common sense is often missing. Nevertheless, we always have the option to choose the higher or lower path.

—JOHN C. NEWMAN

Never doubt yourself. Always believe you can, and let life surprise you.

—JOHN C. NEWMAN

In life, speed can be a double-edged sword. To quickly comprehend is admirable, but to hastily reach the end goal without proper due diligence can be detrimental.

—JOHN C. NEWMAN

Realism in life acknowledges the inevitability of obstacles. We must accept that navigating them successfully may not always be feasible.

—JOHN C. NEWMAN

Life will expose individuals who only see things the way they feel they should. Those who are not willing to look at and accept things the way they are will not be able to do what it takes to effect positive change. Do not become overly concerned; this too is their prerogative.

—JOHN C. NEWMAN

Every day is another opportunity for us to reset our clocks.

—ORVILLE S. A. WHITE
(*TAKE THE TIME AND DO IT.*)

In life, forever is very much a reality. However, nothing lasts, and no one will live forever. Our focus should be on the present, facts, and truth. Realism handles itself.

—JOHN C. NEWMAN

Things will happen in our lives that we cannot control. How we handle the challenges is our choice. There is a major difference between making mistakes and making bad decisions. The goal should be to make as few of the latter as possible.

—JOHN C. NEWMAN

Asking questions when you are unsure demonstrates astuteness. Making assumptions, on the other hand, is unwise.

—JOHN C. NEWMAN

Those of us who are given the blessing of reaching our golden years in life may not remember what we did each day, but astutely recall that it took all day to do it.

—JOHN C. NEWMAN

It matters not who we are; in life, dealing with tolls and strife is universal and unavoidable. Prepare yourself.

—JOHN C. NEWMAN

If we are blessed with longevity in life, the happy byproduct that comes with it is old age. When he knocks on our door, it is our choice to let him in right away.

—JOHN C. NEWMAN

It is crucial to recognize the importance of planning. Nevertheless, our immediate attention and efforts should be directed towards protecting the present. In doing so, we are wisely ensuring the well-being of our tomorrow and future.

—JOHN C. NEWMAN

In life, crying over spilled milk is futile. Focus not on the spilling, but direct your efforts toward acquiring another carton of milk.

—JOHN C. NEWMAN

The most valuable doctrines in life are only experienced by living our lives. This is commonly referred to as wisdom, which comes with patience and the passing of time.

—John C. Newman

We must be aware that life's uncontested mystery is time. We will not know what time will bring, and we don't know when what it brings will arrive. Hence the phrase, "Only time will tell."

—John C. Newman

The only thing in life you should be given is a civil greeting. To receive anything else, you need to work for it.

—John C. Newman

It is essential to recognize that life inherently comprises right and wrong. There are no refunds or second chances, and inevitably, there will be regrets.

—John C. Newman

In the overall scheme of things, it is important to be aware of the "who." What is paramount, however, is that you be certain of the truth before decisions are made: what has been done, what is being done, and what is not being done.

—John C. Newman

The simple realism of life is that there are three things that are immutable. We must play life's game; no one wins; and no one knows when it is their time to exit this wonderful world.

—John C. Newman

It may be a disheartening experience when reaching out to share wisdom with loved ones, close friends, and family who refuse to accept counsel. Be aware that, unfortunately, they may not be willing to change their mindsets. Take solace by being vigilant and supportive when needed.

—John C. Newman

Understanding this one element is vital: to not believe in yourself is the first step to failure.

—John C. Newman

In life, judgment and vengeance belong to the Almighty. There are a plethora of other issues deserving your attention and time.

—John C. Newman

We should be aware that it is impossible to make a blind man see. It matters not our intentions; everyone cannot be saved.

—John C. Newman

In life, we cannot ever go back in time. Its consolation is that we get to carry our memories with us.

—John C. Newman

It is crucial that we understand that the good Lord is not selfish or wasteful. He gives these choices to humanity to make.

—JOHN C. NEWMAN

We must never forget that we are playing a starring role in our lives.

—JOHN C. NEWMAN

Every second counts.

—UNKNOWN AUTHOR (TIME IS TOO PRECIOUS TO WASTE.)

There can be no liberty without patriotism.

—JOHN C. NEWMAN

In life, falling down is very much a reality. What matters is that we keep getting up.

—JOHN C. NEWMAN

Life realism: Making the wrong choice can be the right decision.

—JOHN C. NEWMAN

We would only need a lever long enough, a place to stand, and an axis. Then the world could be moved. Technically speaking, in theory, if given everything you need, the impossible can become a possibility.

—JOHN C. NEWMAN

Selfish individuals dream of how life can benefit them. Caring and visionary individuals dream of how life can benefit humanity. We should all strive to be the latter.

—John C. Newman

When dealing with life challenges, understand that theory will, more often than not, take a back seat to the reality of life.

—John C. Newman

We are given life because of God's grace. We grow and prosper because of His blessings. We die because it is His will. These are the true realities of life.

—John C. Newman

Time is humanity's most precious blessing, as well as life's most feared adversary. Time is the way life is measured. Nothing is exempt from aging.

—John C. Newman

It is essential that we understand how simple life truly is. Don't lie, don't cheat, don't steal, don't overlook the facts, and don't make promises you can't keep.

—John C. Newman

Unsolicited stories usually support the storyteller's point of view.

—John C. Newman

3

MATRIMONY

Humanity will forever hold dear the sacred bond of marriage. Throughout our marriage of over 42 years, my wife and I have weathered numerous challenges and savored countless joyful moments. The success of our enduring partnership owes much to unconditional love, mutual respect, trust, and consistently valuing each other above outside opinions.

Make a pact with your spouse or partner to resolve all quarrels and conflicts before leaving home or going to bed at night. You will never forgive yourself if something happens to either of you, and conflict is the last memory of your beloved.

—John C. Newman

The secret to having a lasting relationship is to listen, respect, trust, and love each other.

—John C. Newman

How to spice up your marriage: Ask your spouse or partner for some seasoning.

—John C. Newman

A stately lady shared with my wife: "I have been married to my husband for over sixty years." My wife asked, "Tell me how you did it." The elder woman smiled, gave her a hug, and said precipitously, "Just like you, honey. One day at a time."

—A distinguished mature woman

Entering into marriage, it's essential to understand that there is no user manual or standard operating procedure to consult when challenges arise.

—John C. Newman

It is essential to understand prior to entering the Holy Bond of Matrimony that infatuation, lust, and love are three entirely different things. However, the latter is mandatory.

—JOHN C. NEWMAN

For a husband to have a happy life, he must do whatever it takes to have a happy spouse.

—UNKNOWN AUTHOR
(*REALIZE THAT ALL CHANGES WILL
NEED TO BE MADE BY THE HUSBAND.*)

You know who you think you are. However, if you want to know what sort of person you really are, ask your spouse or partner. Brace yourself.

—JOHN C. NEWMAN

It does not matter how long you have been married. Just understand that no matter what you quarrel about, the husband will always be the culprit.

—JOHN C. NEWMAN

It is crucial to discern between the actions that put us in the dog house and those actions that put us out of the house, as they carry entirely different consequences. The latter will end your marriage.

—JOHN C. NEWMAN

If you think you made the choice when selecting your loving spouse or partner, you are seriously mistaken. They chose you, and when the decision was made, your fate was sealed.

—JOHN C. NEWMAN

How should you treat your disgruntled spouse or partner? With the utmost care.

—JOHN C. NEWMAN

What do you say to your spouse or partner when they inform you that they are upset? A wise person would say, "Nothing at all."

—JOHN C. NEWMAN

A happily married woman is the lady who goes shopping right after work.

—JOHN C. NEWMAN

A happily married man is the guy who goes home right after work.

—JOHN C. NEWMAN

The adage, "Man can't live on bread alone," is real. The truth is, women can't either. However, if a woman wants to lose five or six pounds, she will give it a try. We married these wonderful creatures!

—JOHN C. NEWMAN

While discussing with your adoring wife or partner a topic you wanted kept between the two of you, ask, "Who else knows about this?" If the answer is, "Just a few of my closest friends," rest assured that your business is on the street.

—John C. Newman

The goal is not to understand our wives or partners. What matters is that we love, respect, and live harmoniously with them. That means knowing when to listen, smile, and keep our mouths closed.

—John C. Newman

It takes conflicts, regrets, and many mistakes for a good, loving marriage to make it.

—John C. Newman

A successful marriage takes commitment and understanding from both parties.

—John C. Newman

To be given time off from your honey to-do list, just ask your wonderful wife or significant other to tell you about their day and listen. You will be free the rest of the day!

—John C. Newman

Something pertaining to your sweethearts and fiancés: You will never hear them expel gas until you are married.

—Unknown Author
(*As quiet as it's kept!*)

Ah, to have a husband, wife, boyfriend, girlfriend, or partner who listens and does not give advice…We all have the right to fantasize.

—JOHN C. NEWMAN

For matrimony to be a lasting union, you must hold on tight when times are bad and not let go when things get worse. Marriage is only flawless in dreams and movies.

—JOHN C. NEWMAN

In life, finding your soul mate is ecstasy. Don't ever take them for granted.

—JOHN C. NEWMAN

When we marry, it is critical that our understanding of life be absolute. You will both go through a metamorphosis during your entire marriage. What makes it a lasting union is that you both embrace and do not resist the changes.

—JOHN C. NEWMAN

Loving your spouse or partner is the most important part of your life. Don't ever forget it.

—JOHN C. NEWMAN

Ask yourself this question: "Where would you be without your loving wife or partner?" If the answer is, "All by yourself," count your blessings. You found your soulmate.

—JOHN C. NEWMAN

Husbands, do not fret when your wife or partner scolds you for doing something that upsets them. Say, "I'm sorry," and move on. This will be a constant occurrence.

—John C. Newman

Wives, do not get upset when your husband or partner leaves their clothes lying around. It will only happen once or twice if you pick them up and hide them.

—John C. Newman

The same thing happens in all marriages. What makes your marriage unique is that now it is happening to you.

—John C. Newman

Be mindful that your spouse is not all that comes with marriage. The unknown byproduct is their eclectic luggage, the unpredictable in-laws. Fret not; it will work itself out.

—John C. Newman

When you find yourself pondering the fact that you no longer have all the freedoms you had before that auspicious day you entered into matrimony, you still do, but now you will be told what, how, when, where, and if you can enjoy them.

—John C. Newman

All that matters in marriage is how happy you both make each other.

—John C. Newman

Most of us realize this right away, but for some, it takes a while. Being married to someone who loves you is the best thing that ever happened to us.

—John C. Newman

There are always going to be challenges. That is an intricate part of marriage. Work together, keep loving each other, and stay on course. The challenges will pass.

—John C. Newman

When it comes right down to it, this is all we can do to keep the peace in our marriage. Ascertain when to say, 'Yes, dear,' 'You're right about that', and 'If that's what you would like to do.'

—Unknown Author
(*AND MOST IMPORTANTLY, WHEN TO SAY NOTHING AT ALL.*)

It's crucial for both partners to understand that tempers may flare occasionally, and there might be moments when you don't like each other. Ultimately, the enduring love you share is what truly matters.

—John C. Newman

The key to having a wonderful, lasting union is to always look out for each other.

—John C. Newman

It will make the relationship a lot less stressful when you both understand how to differentiate rhetorical questions.

—John C. Newman

What you get out of marriage is determined by how much love you put into it.

—John C. Newman

Matrimony has endured the test of time. As long as love continues to co-mingle with joy and happiness, your marriage will be secure.

—John C. Newman

When you find your spouse or partner in life, make their wellbeing the most important part of your life.

—John C. Newman

One of the most misunderstood concepts when entering the sacred bond of matrimony is understanding that being the head of the household does not make you the boss.

—John C. Newman

Share with your spouse or partner how precious they are each day you are blessed to be together. The delight and bliss this brings to your lives will be immeasurable.

—John C. Newman

When entering into the holy bond of matrimony, commit to staying married. This will not, by any means, be an easy task. If mutual trust stays in place, your love for each other will nurture itself, and a lasting union will grow.

—John C. Newman

A genuinely happy, successful marriage cannot be described. It can only be lived and enjoyed.

—John C. Newman

Contrary to widely held belief, there is a time when prudence demands you not be truthful with your spouse or partner. If asked, "Do I look fat in this dress or suit?" The answer should always be a resounding "no."

—John C. Newman

The formula for having a loving, caring marriage that will endure is to develop mutual trust in the relationship.

—John C. Newman

All of us want marriage to last forever. We believe in true love and happiness. Things become difficult when the time comes to disagree without a disagreement. Stay the course and let love do what it does.

—John C. Newman

Marriage can be likened to a fifty-yard dash and a marathon. To win either race is exhilarating and joyful. The first is over very quickly; the latter takes considerably more time, effort, and determination to successfully accomplish.

—John C. Newman

Understand first and foremost: you must want to be married. Then you need to do whatever it takes to stay that way.

—John C. Newman

Marriage is a full-time job. What makes it a loving, successful union is to discern from the beginning that working overtime is an everyday requirement.

—John C. Newman

Our spouses are always right, even when they are wrong. The husband is always wrong.

—John C. Newman

Humanity must become aware of the fact that marriage is not for all of us. Everyone does not share the same mindset or is amenable to this age-old philosophy. If you are not prepared to commit and give mutual trust and respect, stay away from matrimony.

—John C. Newman

Once entering the Holy Bond of Matrimony, these questions will become synonymous. "Where have you been?" "Who were you with?" "What did you do?" "How much money did you spend?" It is crucial that each question be answered the same way, with nothing but the truth.

—John C. Newman

Marriage can and will be a lifelong, loving, and endearing experience if you give each other mutual respect. Commit to putting some skin in the game and staying married.

—JOHN C. NEWMAN

The truth is, no one knows if a marriage will survive or fail; only time will tell.

—JOHN C. NEWMAN

In today's world, marriage is being attacked and redefined. Nevertheless, in my world, marriage will never change. I refuse to play the Jedi mind game.

—JOHN C. NEWMAN

A marriage will become whatever the two partners commit to making it. It takes two.

—JOHN C. NEWMAN

A harmonious marriage is not a fifty-fifty split; if it were, nothing would ever get done. There must be constant give-and-take. A relationship that is divided equally will never last.

—JOHN C. NEWMAN

A little trivia: At old age, your spouses will bear a striking resemblance to their parents.

—JOHN C. NEWMAN

Here's an interesting tidbit: it's completely normal for happily married couples to experience disagreements, engage in banter, and occasionally feel upset with one another.

—John C. Newman

To get married will only take an agreement; to stay married will demand your commitment.

—John C. Newman

In marriage, unconditional love means that no matter what happens, you are both committed to staying forever locked in love's blissful embrace.

—John C. Newman

I would be remiss if I did not share this tad bit of information regarding the holy bond of matrimony: In reality, for some, it can also be a horrific experience.

—John C. Newman

Loving each other and enjoying your lives together will make your marriage thrive.

—John C. Newman

Marriage is fickle, indeed. One minute you're kissing, the next you're shouting, and moments later you're hugging and kissing.

—John C. Newman

Definitively speaking, marriage is extremely challenging. However, there is no greater joy than being blessed with a loving, happy one.

—JOHN C. NEWMAN

The formula for matrimony is the same for everyone. Only the participants are different. Your responsibility will be to stay committed.

—JOHN C. NEWMAN

4

SUCCESS

Humanity consistently aspires to the boundless ideals of success. Commitment and perseverance are crucial for attaining success in life. Yet, regrettably, only a handful are ready to undertake the necessary steps to achieve success.

If you open your mind and clearly define your goals, the universe will help you. Being pro-active with a positive attitude will facilitate success.

—JOHN AND DANELIA NEWMAN

Education alone will not ensure success. The ability to employ common sense is essential.

—JOHN C. NEWMAN

The proper attitude is extremely important when it comes to achieving success.

—JOHN C. NEWMAN

Shape your mind and attitude to meet the challenges of the future, and you will have the tools to achieve success in the present.

—JOHN C. NEWMAN

Most of our successes and failures in life are created by the choices we make. Improve upon your choices, and you will increase the number of your successes.

—JOHN C. NEWMAN

Having a positive attitude is the key to life. Being creative while taking positive actions will unlock doors, and success will be unavoidable.

—JOHN C. NEWMAN

We succeed because of our commitment to achieving our goals. We fail only if we stop believing and lose focus.

—JOHN C. NEWMAN

This is said to be a success formula: $A = X + Y + Z$. X is work. Y is play. Z: Keep your mouth shut. So why not use it, say nothing, and enjoy your success?

—JOHN C. NEWMAN

In the quest for success, imagination and dedication often outweigh our abilities.

—JOHN C. NEWMAN

Neither success nor failure is final or fatal. It is our courage to continue that counts. Never place restraints on yourself. Let the sky be the limit.

—JOHN C. NEWMAN

Being open to the experiences of our predecessors is wise, as it can help us avoid repeating their mistakes.

—JOHN C. NEWMAN

If you are to succeed, it is essential that you are prepared to actually do something to make it happen.

—JOHN C. NEWMAN

Thoughts of Wisdom

Be who you need to be; do what you need to do; and you will have what you need to have. This is also a formula for success.

—John C. Newman

You must be aware of change and transition. It can be the beginning of an opportunity presenting itself to ensure your success.

—John C. Newman

To build an admirably successful team, you must first be a superlative team member. Be conscious of the fact that we must often follow to effectively lead.

—John C. Newman

Developing and implementing your plan of action is a necessity if you want to succeed.

—John C. Newman

Believing in yourself and commitment are two key factors when it comes to achieving success.

—John C. Newman

Becoming successful can be likened to being treated with Novocain. Make your plan, work on it, stay committed, and give it time. It'll work.

—John C. Newman

Successful men and women in life are well informed. And, most importantly, they are willing to act.

—John C. Newman

Committing to doing whatever it takes in life as well as in business will make becoming successful a certainty.

—John C. Newman

Our life situations can be a major factor in the pursuit of success; however, ultimately, what we are willing to do governs our finding it.

—John C. Newman

During your quest to achieve success, the way you present yourself will be most crucial.

—John C. Newman

Visualize your success. Develop a comprehensive action plan and dedicate yourself fully to its implementation; then, get ready to rejoice in your achievements!

—John C. Newman

Listening to successful individuals who possess what we aspire to achieve is crucial, and remaining teachable and open to change is fundamental. By adopting these philosophies, we can make success inevitable.

—John C. Newman

If you are to succeed, it is essential that you are prepared to actually do something to make it happen.

—JOHN C. NEWMAN

Be who you need to be; do what you need to do; and you will have what you need to have. This is also a formula for success.

—JOHN C. NEWMAN

You must be aware of change and transition. It can be the beginning of an opportunity presenting itself to ensure your success.

—JOHN C. NEWMAN

To build an admirably successful team, you must first be a superlative team member. Be conscious of the fact that we must often follow to effectively lead.

—JOHN C. NEWMAN

Developing and implementing your plan of action is a necessity if you want to succeed.

—JOHN C. NEWMAN

Believing in yourself and commitment are two key factors when it comes to achieving success.

—JOHN C. NEWMAN

Becoming successful can be likened to being treated with Novocain. Make your plan, work on it, stay committed, and give it time. It'll work.

—John C. Newman

Successful men and women in life are well informed. And, most importantly, they are willing to act.

—John C. Newman

Committing to doing whatever it takes in life as well as in business will make becoming successful a certainty.

—John C. Newman

Our life situations can be a major factor in the pursuit of success; however, ultimately, what we are willing to do governs our finding it.

—John C. Newman

During your quest to achieve success, the way you present yourself will be most crucial.

—John C. Newman

Imagine that you can achieve success. Create a plan of action and commit to giving it your all; then, prepare to celebrate your success.

—John C. Newman

It is imperative that you focus, take your time, and not rush. Being accurate on the road to becoming successful is paramount.

—John C. Newman

Having a positive attitude, showing respect to others, being a generous giver, and being an excellent receiver while committing to staying focused will guide you to success.

—John and Danelia Newman

To be successful in life, we must trust ourselves. Not believing in yourself is the first secret to failure.

—John C. Newman

To be successful, your ability to have good relationships with others will be crucial.

—John C. Newman

All that life has to offer is there for the taking. Believe that you deserve it. Commit to taking constant positive action, and a myriad of successes will follow.

—John C. Newman

You must be committed to your goals. Achievement begins with that belief.

—John C. Newman

We are all endowed with the ability to achieve. The dilemma is learning to unlock this creativity we have, put it to work, and succeed.

—John C. Newman

To achieve extraordinary results, you should not only think outside the box, but you must also be prepared to step outside the box.

—John C. Newman

Positive thinking and having a vivid imagination keep you moving forward. Taking constant positive action will ensure you succeed.

—John C. Newman

Keeping your eyes open is not enough to take full advantage of opportunities. What is essential is looking in the right direction and taking suitable action if you are to succeed.

—John C. Newman

Do not put the keys to your success in someone else's pocket.

—Unknown Author (*The success is yours.*)

If you are worried about how things will work out in your life, stop. Check your attitude, set goals, plan, and take actions to achieve them. You will be successful.

—John C. Newman

Thoughts of Wisdom

Understand the importance of preparedness and presentation. When given the chance to present your case, it is vital to your success that you are prepared and ready to take full advantage of the opportunity.

—JOHN C. NEWMAN

It has been said that attitude, not aptitude, will determine your altitude. This includes your success.

—JOHN C. NEWMAN

A simple plan to help improve success with finances is to limit expenditures, maintain a budget, and make it a habit.

—JOHN C. NEWMAN

The keys to success are: have a positive attitude, plan, act, be committed, use your imagination, and be pro-active. Now, what else can you think of doing?

—JOHN C. NEWMAN

There are no tricks to successfully getting out of financial strife and staying out. The tried-and-proven formula is to stop spending money you do not have.

—JOHN C. NEWMAN

You will become more efficient if you learn to say, "No." You will become more productive and successful when you realize you should not aid everyone in completing their tasks.

—JOHN AND DANELIA NEWMAN

Getting to know people is just as essential to success as getting to know your job.

—JOHN C. NEWMAN

Life can be capricious; the better candidate may not get the job. Occasionally, what matters is that you show up. This is the realism of life's successes.

—JOHN C. NEWMAN

It is not essential for you to be the best at everything you do. However, it is imperative that you always give your best at everything you do. Your success depends on it.

—JOHN C. NEWMAN

The good news about your journey to becoming successful is that the foremost obstacle you will encounter is yourself.

—JOHN C. NEWMAN

One of the easiest things in life is to find someone or something to blame. Do not squander your time. Focus, take corrective action, and achieve success.

—JOHN C. NEWMAN

The harsh truth is that failure is inevitable for those who opt to give up. To achieve success, remove the phrase "give up" from your vocabulary.

—JOHN C. NEWMAN

Standards, or self-worth, can never be set too high. However, goals and self-esteem can be set too low.

—JOHN C. NEWMAN

First impressions are crucial when meeting people and establishing rapport. They are one-chance items and dramatically increase the odds of success. You will not have a second chance to make one.

—JOHN C. NEWMAN

Change will often be another form of creating opportunity. Embrace it, and succeed.

—JOHN C. NEWMAN

The art of making good decisions goes hand in hand with making bad ones. The key to succeeding is to concentrate on making fewer of the latter and being accountable.

—JOHN C. NEWMAN

Leaders have vision, compassion, honor, and integrity. They are not always liked. However, successful leaders are cognizant of the fact that it is essential that they are respected, not liked.

—JOHN C. NEWMAN

The pinnacle of teaching is when the pupil learns without knowing he or she is being taught. Upon reaching this plateau, achieving success will be inevitable.

—JOHN C. NEWMAN

Motivation comes in many forms. No matter what it is that motivates you, make it a habit. Achieving success will also become one.

—John C. Newman

Do not allow yourself to accept mediocrity. Do not allow those with negative views to distract you. Stay motivated and enthusiastic. You will achieve your goals and succeed.

—John C. Newman

Have a life strategy and make the best of your time. Mistakes can occur by moving too fast or too slowly. Pace yourself, stay on task, seek help if needed, evaluate, analyze, and be aware of your position. Focus on your goals. Success is waiting for you to achieve it.

—John and Danelia Newman

Teamwork manifests itself and thrives when there is a shared goal. It enhances the chances of achieving success.

—John C. Newman

The goal of having what you want in life can be achieved by helping others get what they want. If we all work together, we can all have what we want.

—John C. Newman

Negotiation is an intricate part of life and should be based on respect and creating relationships. When effective negotiating occurs, both sides are content, and the outcome is successful.

—John C. Newman

Words create negative or positive emotions. It is essential that you employ the right words, as they create pictures in your mind. The more vivid the picture, the more effective the communication, and the more likely you are to succeed.

—JOHN C. NEWMAN

Never in the annals of time has change and growth been so rapid. Becoming technologically literate will aid immensely in your pursuit of success.

—JOHN C. NEWMAN

Whether or not you succeed in becoming successful is determined by what you are willing to do.

—JOHN C. NEWMAN

We must embrace and become adept with computer technology in order to succeed in today's world, or we will not be able to compete in the workplace now or tomorrow.

—JOHN C. NEWMAN

Having average employees is not the formula for creating a thriving, successful business. The goal is to always search for someone phenomenal. Average is never successful.

—JOHN C. NEWMAN

In life's journey, we are fortunate if, along the way, we come to the realization that it is not the how that matters. It is our determination and commitment that make us succeed.

—JOHN AND DANELIA NEWMAN

The key to knowledge is observation, comprehension, and experience. The key to success is utilizing them efficiently.

—JOHN C. NEWMAN

To be successful in life, preparation is essential. Success has always favored the committed, the bold, and those who are prepared to receive it.

—JOHN C. NEWMAN

If you feel overwhelmed, continue to focus on the goal and prioritize. Organizing your thoughts will keep you on purpose, and success will eventually reveal itself.

—JOHN C. NEWMAN

How many times can I fail? The answer is… as many times as it takes to succeed.

—JOHN C. NEWMAN

No matter where you go in life, there will always be naysayers. Leave them where you find them and achieve success.

—JOHN C. NEWMAN

In your pursuit of success, stay away from these two emotions: envy and jealousy.

—JOHN C. NEWMAN

Attitude, rather than aptitude, is the chief ingredient for success. Imagination and decisive actions, coupled with desire, will keep you on course and create your success.

—JOHN AND DANELIA NEWMAN

Presentation is crucial when it comes to succeeding. How it is said is just as important as what is said.

—JOHN C. NEWMAN

Knowing yourself is enlightenment; doing whatever it takes yields success.

—JOHN C. NEWMAN

Have the courage to pursue your dreams. Your courage will lead you to success.

—JOHN C. NEWMAN

When imagination, commitment, and dedication are applied, nothing is impossible.

—JOHN C. NEWMAN

Do not allow negative thoughts to enter your mind. They are pessimistic weeds that strangle your self-esteem, confidence, and will to succeed.

—John C. Newman

It will be impossible for you to become successful without your own consent.

—John C. Newman

Before we can make changes in our lives, we must first admit to ourselves that we want change. This includes making the changes necessary to become successful.

—John C. Newman

When it comes to the fine art of negotiation, the rule of thumb is that it is prudent to sacrifice tomorrow's speculations to succeed in closing agreeable negotiations today.

—John C. Newman

It is essential that you consistently plan. If not, you will end up akin to those who do not: unprepared, lacking, and unsuccessful.

—John C. Newman

To dream is one of our most precious blessings. If we are to realize our dreams of success, we must commit to taking the actions needed to achieve them.

—John and Danelia Newman

When we dream big, we win or lose big. When we dream small, we win or lose it all.

—JOHN C. NEWMAN

Accumulating assets is only half the battle. Having those assets generate the desired sustained residual income is becoming successful and winning the war.

—JOHN C. NEWMAN

Creativity, coupled with innovative technology, sound judgment, and hands-on expertise, is a confirmed recipe for success.

—JOHN C. NEWMAN

What matters when you retire is your residual income and quality of life.

—JOHN C. NEWMAN

In life, your success is yours to create. You make it happen, or it never will.

—JOHN C. NEWMAN

Never belittle what you do, and no one will criticize who you are. By belittling what you do, your quest for success will become difficult at best.

—JOHN C. NEWMAN

Time is our most precious commodity. In order to be successful, we must use it efficiently and not take it for granted. Tomorrow is never a foregone conclusion.

—John C. Newman

You must do what is necessary to succeed in order to have what you want in life.

—John C. Newman

Successful individuals do not focus on what they have done. They unwaveringly concentrate on what to do next.

—John C. Newman

To improve your chances of success, you must remain aware of the fact that behavior is taught.

—John C. Newman

We must understand the concept of making mistakes. It enhances our ability to become exceptional and successful.

—John C. Newman

If you become passionate about becoming successful, it will surprise you.

—John C. Newman

If you are willing to give your all, there is very little you can't achieve.

—JOHN C. NEWMAN

The art of being tactful is indispensable when it comes to negotiating and making a point without making an adversary. It also makes it easier to succeed.

—JOHN C. NEWMAN

Do not challenge the wisdom of common sense if your goal is to succeed in becoming successful.

—JOHN C. NEWMAN

We should never give up. There is a close division between success and failure. Your success is usually just a matter of time.

—JOHN C. NEWMAN

What we know is all we know, so we must not get in the way of the universe enriching our lives by not being open to change. It is the gateway to success.

—JOHN C. NEWMAN

Successful people never spend time worrying about what others are doing.

—UNKNOWN AUTHOR
(*THIS IS A PRIMARY REASON FOR THEIR SUCCESS.*)

There are always two sides to every story. Be sure you hear them both before making decisions or drawing conclusions. Your success depends on it.

—JOHN C. NEWMAN

One initiative-taking individual has much more value than several individuals who are only interested. Taking action brings success.

—JOHN C. NEWMAN

"May I, please?" "Thank you very much." "You're welcome." Incorporate these simple phrases into your daily communications, and your world will change dramatically.

—JOHN C. NEWMAN

Do not be an enemy to yourself. Be your best ally and become successful.

—JOHN C. NEWMAN

Change brings knowledge and opportunities. Change also enhances our ability to succeed.

—JOHN C. NEWMAN

Differences are probable and should be expected. Right and wrong are constants and must not be ignored. Success will depend on your choices.

—JOHN C. NEWMAN

Waking up is the easy part. Getting up, going out, and doing something to make a positive contribution is the hard part. Do so, and success will follow.

—JOHN C. NEWMAN

Do not dream your life away. That is way too much time wasted sleeping.

—JOHN C. NEWMAN

Have faith in God and focus on right and wrong. Use these as guides. Most choices and decisions you make will be correct, and your possibilities of success will increase dramatically.

—JOHN C. NEWMAN

We are all biased. Do your best not to let it influence your choices and decisions.

—JOHN C. NEWMAN

It is important to understand when to stop arguing and let that person be wrong.

—UNKNOWN AUTHOR
(*BE AWARE THAT YOU CAN FIND BETTER USE FOR YOUR TIME.*)

When all is said and done, success comes down to attitude and commitment.

—JOHN C. NEWMAN

If you understand that we are responsible for ourselves but are not by ourselves in life, becoming successful will be simpler.

—John C. Newman

We must be ready to take advantage of opportunities. Success is on its way!

—John C. Newman

Every day brings new situations and boundless opportunities, as well as a myriad of pitfalls. Focus on the positive, but be mindful of the negative. Your success depends on it.

—John and Danelia Newman

If you are prepared to go the extra mile, the odds of your success will quadruple.

—John C. Newman

It has been implied that imagination could be more important than knowledge. This is true to a point. Imagination is the first step to success.

—John C. Newman

All that is needed to succeed in life is your belief and unwavering commitment.

—John C. Newman

Thoughts of Wisdom

"Success" and "successful" can be likened to pronouncing the word "tomato." How they are pronounced matters, not when gathering ingredients to prepare the soup.

—John C. Newman

Those who are willing to prepare themselves and stay on course usually succeed.

—John C. Newman

If you just commit to keep moving forward, success will surprise you.

—John C. Newman

To achieve success, you must be willing to move outside of your comfort zone.

—John C. Newman

To succeed in becoming successful, you must first assume you can.

—John C. Newman

Where we place our attention and energy creates results. Our success will not be far behind.

—John C. Newman

It is crucial to verify before acting. It definitely increases your chances for success.

—John C. Newman

Success can be found if you are willing to prepare yourself and pursue it.

—John C. Newman

The only way to ensure you are not going to be a success is to stop trying.

—John C. Newman

Generally, successful people are well informed and make astute decisions.

—John C. Newman

What is important in the formula for success is getting along with people. Without them, there would be no success.

—John C. Newman

Achieving success will not be as easy as giving up. Stay the course and succeed.

—John C. Newman

Your success is only as important as your motivation to achieve it.

—John C. Newman

Decide to become successful, and you are halfway there. Then commit to working toward your plan of action and succeeding.

—John C. Newman

Success is out there waiting for you to come and find it, so begin your search.

—John C. Newman

Success does not always mean happiness. However, it usually brings joy to our lives.

—John C. Newman

Becoming successful in life for some teeters on fanaticism. It is important that in our journey to achieve success, we be mindful of what we are willing to do.

—John C. Newman

As long as you embrace the power of suggestion and imagination, success will never be out of reach.

—John C. Newman

Your success will start and end with the same positive belief.

—John C. Newman

If you commit, trust, focus, and stay on course, you will succeed.

—John C. Newman

There is nothing easy about becoming successful in life. However, there is a simple formula to make it happen: hard work and determination.

—John C. Newman

Becoming successful in life is up to you. It is just that straightforward.

—JOHN C. NEWMAN

Your success depends on how badly you want it and what you are willing to do.

—JOHN C. NEWMAN

Life circumstances are forever changing. In our quest to achieve success, decision-making will be crucial.

—JOHN C. NEWMAN

Success will always embrace hard work and reward smart work.

—JOHN C. NEWMAN

If being successful is your goal, the only sure way not to achieve it is to give up.

—JOHN C. NEWMAN

Success demands work, and to become successful, you will need to work at it.

—JOHN C. NEWMAN

The contrast between being successful or not is simply a lack of willingness to act.

—JOHN C. NEWMAN

The keys to our success can be found by first waking up, then getting out of bed and taking action.

—JOHN C. NEWMAN

Success wears many hats. You need to decide which one you would like to put on.

—JOHN C. NEWMAN

Life is filled with people who gave up on trying to achieve success. Life is also filled with a plethora of successful individuals who did not give up. Choose to be the latter.

—JOHN C. NEWMAN

Success will always be there. It is your choice whether to achieve it or not.

—JOHN C. NEWMAN

Success may not be happiness, but happiness is the key to success. Loving what you do means being successful and making a dream come true.

—JOHN C. NEWMAN

To succeed in life, you must first imagine that you can succeed and envision it happening.

—JOHN C. NEWMAN

You cannot be successful by simply saying you want it and taking no action.

—JOHN C. NEWMAN

Success is comparative. We each have our own ambitions. However, what is universal in life is that it takes work to achieve it.

—JOHN C. NEWMAN

Realize that success is not worth the cost of losing your honor or integrity.

—JOHN C. NEWMAN

The distinction between successful people and those who are not is commitment.

—JOHN C. NEWMAN

Success in your life can only be accomplished by you making it happen.

—JOHN C. NEWMAN

It is understood that becoming successful takes work and commitment. What is sometimes overlooked is that success also demands that you want it.

—JOHN C. NEWMAN

The fear of success can be just as intense as the determination to succeed.

—JOHN C. NEWMAN

Achieving success can be a good or bad thing. It will depend on the individual.

—JOHN C. NEWMAN

What makes success so unique is that it will wait until you are ready.

—JOHN C. NEWMAN

Success is about achievers versus non-achievers; the world is full of both. The decision is yours to make.

—JOHN C. NEWMAN

If you want to become successful, all you need to do is replace "want" with "be."

—JOHN C. NEWMAN

There will always be unsuccessful and successful people. The secret is that the latter individuals worked hard, stayed focused, and achieved it.

—JOHN C. NEWMAN

My success was a dream that included enjoying life and aiding in the well-being of others. Committing to this concept aided immensely in my achieving it.

—John C. Newman

You and procrastination are your number one adversaries for not becoming successful.

—John C. Newman

In life, humanity has always experienced degrees of financial success. All things being considered equal, you have the choice as to which degree of financial success you achieve.

—John C. Newman

Ask yourself, "Why am I not successful?" If you can answer this question, there is no good reason for you not to.

—John C. Newman

It is essential to recognize that while success remains a dream for some, it can become a reality for others. The choice to make it your reality is yours alone.

—John C. Newman

Those of us who succeed in life become ardent about making it happen. Becoming successful is the reward we receive for our industrious efforts.

—John C. Newman

Life grants us initial success with our safe arrival. Whether we achieve further success largely depends on the choices we make and the blessings we receive.

—JOHN C. NEWMAN

The realism in life when it comes to success is that it is attainable for anyone who is willing to achieve it.

—JOHN C. NEWMAN

Above all, it is essential to recognize that we all have the potential to achieve success and become successful in life.

—JOHN C. NEWMAN

When put in simple terms, achieving success will depend on imagination, desire, commitment, and you.

—JOHN C. NEWMAN

The Almighty gives us life and the ability to make choices. To be successful is the task we must accomplish.

—JOHN C. NEWMAN

Our imagination creates dreams. Dreams, action, commitment, and perseverance create our success.

—JOHN C. NEWMAN

Success is straightforward. A person becomes successful through a deliberate effort to attain it. If you decide to pursue success with the same determination, it stands to reason that you can achieve it.

—John C. Newman

Once we realize the power of the conscious and unconscious mind and how they contribute to achieving the success we desire, we grasp that the process to that achievement was an all-day and night production.

—John C. Newman

Success and becoming successful in life are comparative, but the blissful feeling is the same for all those who achieve it.

—John C. Newman

There are many degrees of success in life. It is our choice how successful we would like to become.

—John C. Newman

It is crucial that we not let our failures or successes in life define who we are.

—John C. Newman

5

LOVE

Love is considered a benevolent gift from God to humanity. It stands unrivaled in life, and its power defies understanding. A world devoid of love would be unbearably harsh. For those still seeking love, the quest must continue undeterred.

Love is unpredictable, complicated, bittersweet, and worth all the headaches.

—John C. Newman

How do you let a person know you are in love with them? Ask them to marry you.

—John C. Newman

Our most cherished blessing is finding someone to love who will love you back.

—John C. Newman

It is said that love is blind. I suppose it's because we never see it coming.

—John C. Newman

Individuals in love are one of the most powerful forces in the universe. There is nothing they wouldn't do to protect their love.

—John C. Newman

It only takes a moment to say, "I love you," to your spouse or partner. Take a moment and say it.

—John C. Newman

Men need things in their lives to be logical and just make sense. Women, on the other hand, just need things. And love is needed by all.

—John C. Newman

The reason men and women spend so much time trying to figure each other out is because love is worth all the time spent trying to find it and too precious to lose.

—John C. Newman

Love is a splendorous thing, but only if the feeling of splendor is mutual.

—John C. Newman

There are those who argue that there can be nothing more powerful than the mind. They have underestimated the power of love.

—John C. Newman

How do you surprise a man? Just give him something. He will love it.

—John C. Newman

True love means caring for someone more than life itself.

—John C. Newman

There is no such thing as an unattractive person. There are only some people who are more captivating than others. Love is blind.

—JOHN C. NEWMAN

The phrase "Beauty is in the eye of the beholder" means beauty is in everyone's eye, and every eye loves to see it.

—JOHN C. NEWMAN

It is said that love enters a man through his eyes and a woman through her ears. In that case, we must be particularly vigilant about where we look and what we say. Love is watching and listening.

—JOHN C. NEWMAN

Just how difficult can it be to find true love? Extremely. Just ask any divorcée.

—JOHN C. NEWMAN

Take every opportunity to hug your loved ones and individuals who are dear to you.

—JOHN C. NEWMAN

How long does it take to fall in love? In my humble opinion, the answer to this age-old question would be: As long as it takes.

—JOHN C. NEWMAN

We should thank the Almighty for every day we are given to reach out to our loved ones to share our love.

—John C. Newman

To speak to the hearts of our loved ones and others, we must have love in our hearts.

—John C. Newman

Filling our lives with love, joy, and happiness is as close to life's cure as we can get.

—John C. Newman

Love is what love is, and what a wonderful blessing it is to those who find it.

—John C. Newman

What is love? What can it do for me? The answer to these questions can only be given by those in love, or those who have loved and lost.

—John C. Newman

"I love you" is the most disingenuously used phrase in any language.

—John C. Newman

In the pursuit of love, it is prudent not to lead with your heart; it is too easily broken.

—John C. Newman

Love with all your heart and soul. It is the only way to be sure your love is pure and true.

—JOHN C. NEWMAN

The gift of love is the most sought-after and elusive treasure in life. Individuals who find it are committed and truly blessed.

—JOHN C. NEWMAN

Love and wisdom are time-sensitive achievements. Be mindful that the latter has a much longer incubation period.

—JOHN C. NEWMAN

Love and compassion are all that are needed in our lives to make it worth living.

—JOHN C. NEWMAN

Hug, kiss, and tell your spouse or partner you love them every day.

—JOHN C. NEWMAN

True love is: When things go wrong, and they will, you just keep trying.

—JOHN C. NEWMAN

Love is likened to the taste of sugar. You can only say it is sweet, but you cannot describe it.

—JOHN C. NEWMAN

Understanding the distinction between loving someone and being in love with someone is crucial, as they are two completely different experiences.

—JOHN C. NEWMAN

If you believe love is free of pain or conflict, you are in for a big surprise!

—JOHN C. NEWMAN

Love can be simple, complicated, and, at times, very confusing. Do not try to understand it. Just smile and enjoy its splendor.

—JOHN C. NEWMAN

Falling in love can be likened to attending a magic show. When it is over, "Abracadabra," you're in love.

—JOHN C. NEWMAN

When you find true love, all you can think about is, "Why did it take so long?"

—JOHN C. NEWMAN

Two people who are in love will always be in love. Things become unmanageable if you are unwilling to do whatever it takes or forget why you're together.

—JOHN C. NEWMAN

Falling in love means not being able to focus on anything but that person. Oh, what a feeling!

—John C. Newman

The closest panacea to life's challenges is living with unconditional love in our lives.

—John C. Newman

Without love, the world would be plunged into total chaos.

—John C. Newman

To be content with our spouse, partner, or significant other and happy with the life we lead is to live in love's embrace.

—John C. Newman

"When love calls and the phone rings, it will always be answered."

—Unknown Author (*It is mandatory.*)

Are you happy? Can you live without this person in your life? If you answer these questions with a "yes" and a "no," consider yourself in love.

—John C. Newman

Love is so precious that wars have been fought over it. Do not underestimate its power.

—John C. Newman

Having loving parents, family, and friends is the ultimate love experience.

—John C. Newman

You must love yourself first, or you will not appreciate or accept the love of anyone else.

—John C. Newman

Love is a mystery that has joyfully bewildered humanity since its creation and will not ever stop.

—John C. Newman

When love is in your life, everyone you meet can see it. And if they don't, you tell them.

—John C. Newman

If you continually think about that person, often dream about that person, and always want to be with that person, you are in love. Oh, and you have a hefty dose of it!

—John C. Newman

Mutual trust is the reason that true love survives and thrives.

—John C. Newman

The question has been asked, "What's love got to do with it?" The answer is everything!

—John C. Newman

It is crucial that we be aware that love and happiness are not synonymous.

—JOHN C. NEWMAN

Love is the only entity in life that wears two hats. It passionately embraces both good and evil, abetting each with equal zeal.

—JOHN C. NEWMAN

What makes love so miraculous is that when it happens, we do not know how or why, but we are extremely grateful it did.

—JOHN C. NEWMAN

Love never disappoints; the challenge is for those individuals who do not treat it with the respect it deserves.

—JOHN C. NEWMAN

The only thing in life that humanity can totally agree on is how wonderful love is.

—JOHN C. NEWMAN

Love can be likened to an undefeated prize fighter. From the beginning of time, it has taken on any and all challengers and still reigned supreme.

—JOHN C. NEWMAN

For love to grow and thrive, there has to be space in the heart. Make sure there is enough room in yours for love to flourish.

—JOHN C. NEWMAN

Love never dies; only those we love do.

—JOHN C. NEWMAN

Once love chooses you, there is nothing you can do to avoid it, and you wouldn't want to.

—JOHN C. NEWMAN

Love is frightening but wonderful at the same time. We lose total control, and we love it!

—JOHN C. NEWMAN

There has never been anyone who has had too much love, and there never will be anyone.

—JOHN C. NEWMAN

Love will always be out there in the universe, lingering. All we need to do is make it our passion to find it. God willing, we will receive its blessing.

—JOHN C. NEWMAN

Love's mystery has endured the annals of time and will forever continue to do so.

—JOHN C. NEWMAN

When both spouses or partners give each other unconditional love, it epitomizes living in life's loving embrace.

—JOHN C. NEWMAN

Love and beauty are inseparable. Love and being loved are heaven-sent and a joy to behold.

—JOHN C. NEWMAN

Love is so remarkable that we can be in love and not know it!

—JOHN C. NEWMAN

In life, some may think they are in love; others say they might be in love. If there is any doubt, the answer is that it is definitely not love; it is most likely a crush, infatuation, or lust.

—JOHN C. NEWMAN

Love is priceless; it is given to humanity, and we are all so blessed for it. If love wasn't blind, there would be millions of people still standing in line waiting to enjoy its splendor.

—JOHN C. NEWMAN

When it comes to true love, it doesn't matter who is right or wrong; you stay together and work it out. And continue loving each other.

—JOHN C. NEWMAN

There are a plethora of things in life that humanity can live without. Love is not one of them.

—John C. Newman

Falling in love can be likened to eating ice cream and cake, just as losing love can be likened to eating a lemon or a lime. The latter two leave you with a bitter, sour taste.

—John C. Newman

Love is what love is. Oh, how wonderful it is!

—John C. Newman

6

HAPPINESS

Humanity's eternal quest is the pursuit of happiness. Identifying what brings us joy should be our steadfast goal in life. Knowing what happiness may look like can save a tremendous amount of time.

The true measure of happiness is to always have in our lives things that make us happy.

—John C. Newman

Happiness can be found in the hearts of those who believe in their dreams. It is given to no one. It is achieved by those who have the conviction and courage to act.

—John C. Newman

Once you understand that it is how much you give back that makes the difference, your approach to life will immediately change. The world will instantly become a better place, and joy and happiness will become constants in your life.

—John C. Newman

In life, achieving true happiness means wanting what life has given you. And whatever it turns out to be, you have been blessed.

—John C. Newman

When it comes to money, its value is remarkably close to that of H2O. We can manage a short while without it, but not for very long. Money has the same effect on happiness.

—John C. Newman

Know what is essential to you; then you can be true to yourself and find happiness.

—JOHN C. NEWMAN

The adage, "If you want something done right, do it yourself," is outdated. Pay a professional to do it right and get a receipt. That will make you happy.

—JOHN C. NEWMAN

To be the owner of a 100-foot yacht would be wonderful. On the other hand, you would be just as happy if you had good friends who were proud owners of one.

—UNKNOWN AUTHOR *(CULTIVATE THOSE FRIENDSHIPS.)*

We all seek happiness; however, we will not all achieve it. The reason for this is relatively simple. It depends on our dedication and what we are willing to do.

—JOHN C. NEWMAN

A woman with money can still be miserable. A man with money would simply buy something to make himself happy.

—JOHN C. NEWMAN

Happiness, like everything precious in life, will only be accomplished by the committed.

—JOHN C. NEWMAN

The blueprint to happiness is unsophisticated but not undemanding. You must be willing to do whatever it takes to achieve it.

—JOHN C. NEWMAN

Humor is a vital part of our lives. Its significance can be overlooked. Laughter is a panacea for many of our ills. A life filled with laughter is a life full of joy and happiness.

—JOHN C. NEWMAN

The adage that says, "Seek first to understand and then to be understood" is one of the most valuable pieces of advice ever given. We must also learn to care for each other before we can truly get along and live happily ever after.

—JOHN C. NEWMAN

Aged single malt whisky, fine wine, expensive champagne, beautiful women, dining at six-star restaurants, handsome men, Cuban cigars, fast exotic cars… Oh yes, fantasizing also makes us happy!

—JOHN C. NEWMAN

The spices of life are something we must all resolve for ourselves, or we will never find happiness and enjoy life.

—JOHN C. NEWMAN

The formula for losing weight is simple: exercise and intake fewer calories. But would that make you happy?

—JOHN C. NEWMAN

Arguably, the greatest motivational book ever written is the Bible. It gives us the principles for achieving happiness and success, and it is the road map to get us there.

—JOHN C. NEWMAN

Even a blind squirrel finds a nut once in a while.

—UNKNOWN AUTHOR (*THIS IS HAPPINESS.*)

If the stress in our lives is kept to a minimum, we will be healthier and happier.

—JOHN C. NEWMAN

Focusing on things you missed only takes time away from enjoying those things that make you happy.

—JOHN C. NEWMAN

To find happiness, go out and look for it, and do not come back until you find it.

—JOHN C. NEWMAN

Friends come in two distinct types: fair-weather and lifelong. Do whatever is necessary to make the latter; they will make you happy.

—JOHN C. NEWMAN

Finding happiness takes commitment. If you have some idea of what you are looking for, it will save you an enormous amount of time.

—JOHN C. NEWMAN

Being a good friend is the only way you will appreciate having one, and having a good friend will make you happy.

—John C. Newman

People are not flawless, and the world is not perfect. Learn to forgive, and life will become more pleasurable; with that comes happiness.

—John C. Newman

If we welcome whatever life brings us and are willing to adjust and understand that knowledge will be achieved with the passing of time, achieving the dream of happiness will be just a matter of time.

—John and Danelia Newman

Having happiness in your life is truly a blessing. You must be mindful that it is not to be taken for granted.

—John C. Newman

There is little joy and happiness in life without having someone to share it with.

—John C. Newman

When I was young, I wanted to live forever. Now that I have reached my golden years in life, I just want to live happily for as long as I live.

—John C. Newman

Feeling good should be our everyday goal. Feeling this way should make us all happy.

—John C. Newman

Waking up in the morning and looking forward to enjoying your day is happiness.

—John C. Newman

Happiness is being able to joke and laugh at yourself. What a wonderful virtue!

—John C. Newman

We alone own our happiness. No one can make us happy unless we want them to.

—John C. Newman

Open your heart to others, and be willing to recognize that we all have flaws and will continue to make mistakes. Only then will you be ready for happiness to find you.

—John C. Newman

Happiness, love, and forgiveness are what make the world a wonderful place to live.

—John C. Newman

We all must discern what makes us happy. To achieve it, your effort and will are crucial.

—JOHN C. NEWMAN

The world, its boundaries, and our likes, dislikes, wants, and needs are forever changing. If we want to achieve happiness, our focus on it needs to be consistent.

—JOHN C. NEWMAN

To be happy, you need to be a happy person. If you are a happy person, you will find yourself surrounded by happiness.

—JOHN C. NEWMAN

Those of us who are genuinely happy understand that it was up to us, not anyone else.

—JOHN C. NEWMAN

A genuinely happy person smiles and laughs a lot and has never met a stranger.

—JOHN C. NEWMAN

Happiness will not be found without you being able to trust your fellow man.

—JOHN C. NEWMAN

Being happy is your choice to make, and it can be achieved if you work at it.

—John C. Newman

Happiness means different things to all of us. What makes it amazing is that it feels the same.

—John C. Newman

Everyone would like to be happy; not doing what it takes is why so many are not.

—John C. Newman

Living life the way you want is happiness.

—John C. Newman

Happiness is when most days in your life have been very enjoyable.

—John C. Newman

What makes life worth living is finding happiness and someone to share it with.

—John C. Newman

If you receive the blessing of happiness in your life, do your best not to let it leave.

—John C. Newman

In life, the blessing of being happy is sought after by all. It is achieved and enjoyed by those willing to give as much as we receive in life's journey.

—John C. Newman

Happiness is not sitting on a shelf; it is bestowed on those who have given their all to pursue it.

—John C. Newman

If you find happiness, do not become complacent, or you will find yourself looking for it all over again.

—John C. Newman

Happiness is a universal desire; achieving it is a blessing for those willing to go find it.

—John C. Newman

To find and enjoy the blessing of happiness, we must be deserving first.

—John C. Newman

Rid your life of hatred, bigotry, envy, and jealousy, and love, joy, and happiness will come looking for you.

—John C. Newman

Happiness is a blessing. Once you find it, the challenging job will be to hold on to it.

—John C. Newman

Finding someone who will love you as much as you love them is happiness.

—John C. Newman

Happiness cannot be bought; it is one of the wonderful blessings God bestows on humanity.

—John C. Newman

Finding happiness can be likened to magic. If we do not continue doing what brought it about, it can disappear, and the process of finding it will need to start all over again.

—John C. Newman

The formula to make it possible for us all to find happiness is to commit to doing whatever it takes to achieve it.

—John C. Newman

If happiness were to make itself easier to realize, the world would be an even happier place to live.

—John C. Newman

In life, the divide between being happy and happiness is so miniscule that it would be virtually impossible to live on the difference.

—John C. Newman

It is a well-known fact that you cannot buy happiness. However, it hasn't and will never stop humanity from continuing to try and purchase it.

—John C. Newman

The world would be a very unpleasant place to live without love, joy, and happiness.

—John C. Newman

I changed my mindset, became teachable, gathered wisdom from a plethora of encounters, assimilated all of it, and made it my own. Love, marriage, success, and happiness found me.

—John C. Newman

POEMS DEPICTING LIFE

Poems and stories serve as humanity's means to depict the passage of life. The events of our lives are captured through photographs, notes, letters, and memories, yet poetry remains the most profound embodiment of our experiences.

What happens in life will come to pass.
No matter what we do, our youth will not last.
Try to live each day without regret.
We give the challenges in life our best.

—John C. Newman

Life reflects action and reaction;
It is who we are and what we do.
Give the world the best you have,
And accept what life gives back to you.

—John C. Newman

We are given a chance to make our mark in life.
What it is becomes permanent; you cannot do it twice.
Do not feel sorry for yourself if you fail a test.
Not knowing all the answers, it was prudent to guess.

—John C. Newman

All we have is all we have;
It matters not how much we hope, wish, and dream.
Do not live your life in a fantasy world.
There, nothing is what it seems.

—John C. Newman

The life we live is ours alone.
One day we are here; the next we are gone.
There are many things in life that we cannot control.
Finding love, joy, and happiness should be our goal.

—John C. Newman

One second, one hour, one day—life continues on.
The secret is that our lives may be both short and long.
Life's realism is that we will all pass on someday.
The mystery is how much time we have to stay.

—John C. Newman

On the journey through life, there will be toil and strife.
We hope that most days we enjoy life.
We use our piety and wit to deal with what we find.
It is etched in stone until the end of time.

—John C. Newman

Time never waits for anyone; our task is to survive.
It's a mystery that we have no clue when our time will arrive.
We try to prepare ourselves and handle what it may bring.
Time is the key to all our lives and affects everything.

—John C. Newman

Life teaches its lessons, whether we learn them or not.
Its teachings continue and will never stop.
Life's dilemma stays the same: we do not get to know when
The lessons are over, and our lives will end.

—John C. Newman

We are fortunate to have had one good friend in our lives.
Having two or three, consider yourself blessed.
Stay focused; don't let your search end.
It's no easy task to find a good friend.

—JOHN C. NEWMAN

In life, sometimes we win, and sometimes we lose.
In some situations, we don't get to choose.
There are few do-overs; we usually only get one chance.
Consider yourself lucky; you were invited to the dance.

—JOHN C. NEWMAN

Life has always rewarded the committed, strong, and bold.
Some of us are fortunate and will live to grow old.
Our journey will be perilous, but God's blessing is there to behold.
It is the time He gives those for our story to be told.

—JOHN C. NEWMAN

The circle of life is capricious indeed.
Each day, someone comes and another leaves.
It is the way of life; no one is ever deceived.
Today, families will rejoice, and families will grieve.

—JOHN C. NEWMAN

In the fickle game of life, we all get to play.
Win or lose, it comes as it may.
Prepare yourself the best you can.
When the carousel stops, no one gets to stand.

—JOHN C. NEWMAN

Life will go on one day at a time, no matter the situation.
Some days are pleasant, while others create aggravation.
We must focus on the good and not on the bad.
Being thankful and appreciative of the blessings we have had.

—John C. Newman

To have love in our lives is a wonderful thing.
There is no description of the joy that it brings.
Do all in your power to nurture this love.
And thank the Almighty, for it comes from above.

—John C. Newman

Life can be likened to a rainbow, with its many colors, shades, and hues.
There are as many choices as there are points of view.
What matters are our blessings and what we get to choose.

—John C. Newman

We are brought into the world; we have no say.
Our lives are measured day by day.
The mystery is not knowing where or when
Our lives will end as surely as they began.

—John C. Newman

Some days we are happy; others we are sad.
Enjoy the good times and accept the bad.
We live each day with fond hopes of tomorrow,
Not knowing if life will bring us a day of sweet sorrow.

—John C. Newman

While we journey through life, there will be many choices.
And more so than that, we hear many voices.
Be willing to listen; knowledge is what we are all seeking.
In order to be taught, we must be amenable to the teaching.

—JOHN C. NEWMAN

It is your life; for how long it is unknown.
This information belongs to the Almighty alone.
Accountability is ours to own.
As for tomorrow, life is unknown.

—JOHN C. NEWMAN

The winds of time will continue to blow.
The ocean tides will ebb and flow.
What we reap in life is what we sow.
Life's secret is that no one gets to know
When it is time for them to go.

—JOHN C. NEWMAN

We live life the best we can.
There is a different view from where we individually stand.
Life is precious and cherished by us all.
We live our lives knowing that one day we must fall.

—JOHN C. NEWMAN

We are all enrolled in the school of life.
The curriculum changes from day to day.
What makes life intriguing is that we get to learn and play
As life teaches its lessons every single day.

—John C. Newman

The world is a place where we all live.
What makes life amazing is that we each have something different
    to give.
Our dilemma is that no one gets to know what it is,
Or how much time we have to live.

—John C. Newman

In certain instances in life, it matters less what we say,
But it is crucial to what we do every day.
To justify or blame is a waste of time for you.
It is your life, and accountability belongs to you, too.

—John C. Newman

We all know life's secret; the secret is time.
Its treasures are precious and exhilarating to find.
What is certain is that we are all given a life to live.
And we ask God's blessings, for life is only His to give.

—John C. Newman

The world is brimming with many wondrous things.
Some are pleasant, and some are unpleasant, too.
It depends on our commitment, perspective, and what we are willing
    to do.
How much good or bad is harvested is entirely up to you.

—John C. Newman

Since the beginning of time, life has remained the same.
So, we prepare ourselves to play its capricious game.
We must pay attention as we watch life's show.
The time will come, and each of us must go.

—John C. Newman

The Almighty gifts us life, which begins with the absence of sin.
We acquire transgression as we become adults therein.
How much do we choose to pollute ourselves along the way?
Determines our final destination when life is taken away.

—John C. Newman

What we do today, what we dare to say,
What we are willing to pay, and the time life gives us to stay
Will determine how we handle what the future brings our way.

—John C. Newman

In life, only those who are blessed will see tomorrow.
The time we are given cannot be bought, lent, or borrowed.
We must do all we can to minimize life's sorrow.
No one is promised today or tomorrow.

—John C. Newman

Utopia is but a dream; this we understand.
So, we commit to living our lives the best we can.
Life unfolds the same for each child, woman, and man.
When the sacred horn blows, we must depart this land.

—JOHN C. NEWMAN

Our lives are a search to find who we will grow up to be.
For some, the quest will end before they get to see.
Our given times vary; on this, we will have no say.
When our search time is over, we will fade away.

—JOHN C. NEWMAN

Wake up and act, for time is moving fast.
Life is uncertain; it's a secret how long we will last.
We each have our own mission; we are given different tasks.
There is no time to tarry, for today will swiftly pass.

—JOHN C. NEWMAN

Life is unique as a snowflake; no day is ever the same.
Giving your best is the name of the game.
We can't ever go back to where we came.
So, we go on living life's capricious game.

—JOHN C. NEWMAN

The stories of life will forever be told.
Its tragedies and good fortunes will continue to unfold.
So, we seek the blessing of getting old.
Leaving those behind for our stories to be told.

—JOHN C. NEWMAN

One day at a time is how we must live.
We do our best to enjoy each day He gives.
Life's uncertainty is how long we have to live.

—JOHN C. NEWMAN

Life's journey has a beginning, and ultimately it must end.
We tell our stories of what we have seen and where we have been.
Right implies the good times; wrong denotes the bad.
We take solace in our good fortune and the blessings we have had.

—JOHN C. NEWMAN

Life is wonderful, amazing, and intriguing,
As well as complicated, overwhelming, and confusing.
God's blessings that come with each day He begins
Is a reminder of what a wonderful world we live in.

—JOHN C. NEWMAN

To enjoy life in every way,
We must count each blessing from day to day.
The world goes around; we have no say.
Where our cards fall is where they must stay.

—JOHN C. NEWMAN

In life, each of us will get to choose.
Though you do not get to know if you will win or lose,
His grace is blissful; we get to choose.

—JOHN C. NEWMAN

We live our lives the best we can;
The world is filled with choices.
We choose whichever we think is best,
And cannot change what happens next.

—John C. Newman

Life is a play, and we have the starring role.
Our destiny is something over which we have no control.
Life's secret is that we know not where or when.
What is certain is that it will come to an end.

—John C. Newman

To live life without trust, there would be no us
And we would be living on our own.
Take the time to develop trust,
And don't live your life alone.

—John C. Newman

There are many paths in life that we can take.
There are a plethora of decisions that we must make.
There are many things we can do.
The choices you make are up to you.

—John C. Newman

Understanding who we are is a daunting task.
"Who am I?" is the question you should ask.
Who we thought we were and who we really are may not be who
    we expected,
So embrace life's realism and accept it.

                                   —JOHN C. NEWMAN

The life we live will be joyful and sad;
We must live it, expecting both the good and the bad.
What matters most is the time we have had.

                                   —JOHN C. NEWMAN

This world we live in is tough;
In life, growing up can be rough.
Whom you grow into depends solely on you,
And how well you carry out the tasks that life gives you to do.

                                   —JOHN C. NEWMAN

In life, it matters not who is there;
We live one day at a time, and we are aware
There will be many games along the way,
And like them or not, we all must play.
When our play time ends, no one gets to know;
The certainty in life is that we all must go.

                                   —JOHN C. NEWMAN

As children, the world is amazing and life is so much fun.
We grow up and recognize its dangers, and our play times are done.
Now we must live our lives the best we can,
Handling adult responsibilities and taking a stand.

—JOHN C. NEWMAN

Life can be likened to an exquisite restaurant; we are all chefs in
    life's game.
Each day, our menu must change; it will never be the same.
Life's secret is not knowing if it gets opened, or for how long each day.
This is truly a dilemma in which we will have no say.

—JOHN C. NEWMAN

There are choices in life we have to make;
Each comes with a risk that we must take.
Once we board our train and it leaves the station,
Time will determine our final destination.

—JOHN C. NEWMAN

Life is like the ocean with rough, stormy seas.
Once the storm is over, it's a calm place to be.
Looking back and remembering the why, where, and when,
We enjoy the cruise as it comes to an end.

—JOHN C. NEWMAN

In life, there are different paths we can take,
And a plethora of choices and mistakes to make.
The game of life is simple; we make it complex
When we try to predict its next prospects.

—John C. Newman

Mistakes are made by all of us;
To forgive is what we must do.
In your life, there may come a time
When the person needing forgiveness is you.

—John C. Newman

No one lives life free; it comes with a price.
We live day by day and roll the dice.
When the time arrives to pay life's price,
Will you stand and fight, or will running away suffice?

—John C. Newman

In life, love, joy, success, and happiness are there for us to find.
Some of us accomplish these things if the Lord is kind.
The question is, "Who will be blessed with enough search time?"

—John C. Newman

The circle of life is a carousel that never stops spinning.
What we do and say determines who is winning.
When time expires and it is the end of our day,
The sun goes down, and we fade away.

—John C. Newman

We only have one true life to live;
It is our decision how much we give.
What we get in return along the way
Depends on the time we are given to stay.

—John C. Newman

If each person knew how long they had to live,
We would all be prudent when the time came to give.
Aware of life's secret, we would dread the day,
Waiting for our time to pass away.

—John C. Newman

Life is a production, and the world is our stage.
Rehearsal times will vary, as will the salaries we are paid.
No one knows the answer as to how long or when;
Once the final scene is over, our lives will also end.

—John C. Newman

Our reflection in life's mirror will always be true
If the person looking back does not recognize you.
The dilemma then becomes: What should we do?
Both the reflection and the person are the same; it's you.

—John C. Newman

In life, amassing material things can impress.
Achieving fame and fortune can appear to be success.
Yet, we still may not find love or happiness.

—John C. Newman

There will be trials throughout life's journey,
And we will not pass every test.
When we are unsure of the answers, we can only guess.
Still, lessons must be learned as life's games will never end.
What makes life so exciting is when we get to win.

—John C. Newman

Life does not distribute time equally;
For some, it will give less.
We sit alone in class when life administers its final test,
Taking solace in knowing that we gave our very best.

—John C. Newman

It is said that we can live life twice.
The mind can play tricks on us in an effort to entice.
We astutely understand that illusions are never what they seem.
Our first life is reality; the second is in our dreams.

—John C. Newman

How unique life truly is.
Some parts are challenging, and others are blissful to live.
It depends on our understanding of life
And how much we are willing to give.
Life's unknown stays the same: the time we have to live.

—John C. Newman

How we will be remembered is not the question that should be
    asked.
The most important things in life are the blessings we receive before
    we pass.
Focus should be spent on time with loved ones, not on what we have.
Our memories should be of joyful times and not be wasted on
    the sad.

—John C. Newman

As life begins and we take our first breath,
We move through the circle of life until our eventual death.
The Lord is the keeper of the sacred scroll;
His grace and blessings determine who lives to grow old.

—John C. Newman

Life is like a puzzle, and its pieces are time.
To put it together, each piece we must swiftly find.
We are all placed on a clock to assemble our life-given task.
The mystery is not knowing how long our time will last.

—John C. Newman

The time we have to live our lives is more precious than gold.
We cannot afford to waste a moment; we must be brave and bold.
Life's uncertainty will always be the same;
When the whistle blows, it ends life's game.

—John C. Newman

Life's game is fickle; we know not where its journey leads.
We live for a definitive amount of time, and no one is deceived.
The realism is that we must live our lives and leave.

—JOHN C. NEWMAN

In life, there are those who say they do not want to live.
The Lord is the one who has life to give.
He decides who comes and who lives.

—JOHN C. NEWMAN

Love is a blessing in life from the Almighty to you.
When He puts it in our hearts, love is pure and true.
We all make the same decision; it is what we are compelled to do.
We spend our lives searching for someone special to give our hearts
    and love to.

—JOHN C. NEWMAN

In life, we have a finite amount of time to live.
It is our choice how much of ourselves we decide to give.
Life can be short; we must make our choices fast.
Prudence demands we act quickly, for today may be our last.

—JOHN C. NEWMAN

Our lives will end; we have no say.
Accomplishments in life are there to stay.
Who we met and what we saw as we lived each day
No longer matters after we have passed away.

—JOHN C. NEWMAN

What makes life so amazing is its mixture of sadness and glee.
On many of its options and requirements, we will not agree.
The truth is, often things are not how we would like them to be.
However, in life, reality is always there in plain sight for us to see.

—John C. Newman

The good Lord gives us life and tickets to each of its shows.
We won't all make it to the movies, as He decides who comes and
    goes.
Life's theater has a seating capacity, and what it is, no one gets to
    know.
The certainty is that life's movies end,
And its shows begin all over again.

—John C. Newman

Life will keep changing each and every day.
Making adjustments is crucial, as there is a precious price to pay.
No one is exempt; in time, we all pay life's toll.
Some will need to pay for it early; others will wait until they are old.

—John C. Newman

To live and enjoy life is a universal goal.
It is easier said than done, if the truth be told.
What makes life complex is where its mystery begins;
Our dilemma is never knowing which way life will spin.

—John C. Newman

If life gives us the blessing to reach our golden years,
We should accept the Lord's approval, for it is exactly as it appears.
Our time must be used wisely to graciously teach and give,
For this is surely the reason He selected us to live.

—JOHN C. NEWMAN

For some, life's journey is quick and short;
For others, the path will be long and slow.
It depends on our blessings and how far we have to go,
Or the part we are given to play in life's show.
Life's secret is that no one ever gets to know.

—JOHN C. NEWMAN

8

THE FUTURE: MY OPINIONS

The future is unavoidable, and the accomplishments of humanity will significantly shape it. We understand that the future cannot be halted or delayed. Nevertheless, it is crucial that we seize every opportunity to improve.

Entitlements, being politically correct, fake news—these are a nation and society's "Achilles Heel." If these issues are not dealt with forthwith and continue their present course left unchecked, a daunting future is on the horizon.

—John C. Newman

What is happening in the world today demands humanity's undivided attention. How these challenges are handled is vital to ensuring a thriving future.

—John C. Newman

Today, many individuals feel they are entitled to a share of what someone else has worked for. This mindset is not conducive to today or a prosperous future.

—John C. Newman

To give all that we have is to make the ultimate sacrifice. When the time comes to stand up and fight, too few will have the resolve. The future will suffer a shocking blow.

—John C. Newman

What a fickle, perplexing world we live in. We can do all the unethical and immoral things we want if they are not illegal, giving no thought to future consequences.

—John C. Newman

There will always be those who are willing to listen; it does not matter if you are telling the truth or lying. What gives me pause is that many in today's society would rather hear the latter, giving no concern as to its effect on the future.

—JOHN C. NEWMAN

Accurate, relevant, dependable, and responsible; if the information we give and receive meets these criteria, confusion and misunderstandings will decline, and the future will be auspicious.

—JOHN C. NEWMAN

Being able to apply the common-sense factor is morally indispensable and necessary for humanity to ensure its future well-being.

—JOHN C. NEWMAN

True harmony in the world can only be achieved by humanity's change of mindset from "I" and "them" to "we" and "us." Without trust, unity, and acceptance, a harmonious future is questionable.

—JOHN C. NEWMAN

To make the world a better place to live and secure a strong future, we need to ensure that the gray areas in our lives become negligible and focus on practicality.

—JOHN C. NEWMAN

We need each other. Why is this so problematic for humanity to embrace? We must all become aware of this so as to effect a future of opulence.

—John C. Newman

The future is artificial intelligence (AI); it is advancing rapidly. The achievements are unbelievable. These incredible developments also bring with them perilous, life-threatening responsibilities. Humanity must remain vigilant and judicious.

—John C. Newman

Politics may not be a prudent place for an honest person to consider having a future.

—John C. Newman

It has been said that the world is ours for the taking. This can be a very scary statement, as it places skepticism on the future.

—John C. Newman

History must always be the true story of what happened, etched in stone and never erased, not his story or their story. The past has a resounding effect on the present and the future.

—John C. Newman

Before our situation deteriorates to an "Inferno," it is imperative that humanity unites. Failure to do so may lead to catastrophic consequences in the future.

—John C. Newman

Many times in life, after losing a debate, slander becomes the tool of the losers. The future suffers.

—JOHN C. NEWMAN

Those who control the world's debt also control the world and its future. This should give our society grave concern.

—JOHN C. NEWMAN

We survive to see the future only if we learn to love and care for each other, starting yesterday.

—JOHN C. NEWMAN

Modern-day slaves are not in chains. They are in debt.

—UNKNOWN AUTHOR
(SADLY, SO WILL BE THE FUTURE.)

Humanity's future challenges will not be about nuclear mismanagement. They will be about a disease called "ineptocracy" (in-ep-toc'-ra-cy). Political inept.

—JOHN C. NEWMAN

Humanity should dread the day that technology surpasses our human interaction. The future, at best, will become frightening.

—JOHN C. NEWMAN

Society's reluctance to be amenable to opposing points of view is not conducive to ensuring a healthy future.

—John C. Newman

The future and our existence are joined at the hip. Humanity's mindset must change dramatically if we are expecting the future to be inhabitable and affluent.

—John C. Newman

We are all different, yet so much alike, and the future hinges on our ability to get along.

—John C. Newman

Good and evil have and always will be the world's dilemma. Humanity's choices will determine this conflicting outcome, and the future depends on making informed ones.

—John C. Newman

Without the existence of patriotism and a commitment to bipartisanship in government, a country's as well as society's future is questionable.

—John C. Newman

For our country to ensure a secure future, we must return to the mindset of the lyrics of our Star-Spangled Banner.

—John C. Newman

Since the beginning of time, there has been a struggle for world dominance. Several have tried and failed, and each time humanity paid a horrendous cost. Have we learned nothing from this age-old quest? Our nature seems to seek conflict and destruction rather than harmony for the future.

—John C. Newman

Observing humanity's trials conveys concerns about the future. We are overlooking the significance of teaching our youth the basic essentials. Instead, we are allowing them to become dependent solely on technology and the opinions of others. While advances are indispensable and counsel is valued, so is the ability to think for ourselves and employ common sense.

—John C. Newman

When society's accountability is out to lunch and if its responsibility does not return forthwith, the future's wellbeing will be seriously questionable and challenged.

—John C. Newman

Laws, rules, and consequences are put in place for a purpose; they are immutable when it comes to protecting society and the country. When blatantly disregarded, only undesirable outcomes and detriments are on the horizon. The future becomes grim.

—John C. Newman

It is crucial for those making decisions that affect countries and humanity's future to first be judicious and aware of the ramifications of their actions. The future hangs in the balance.

—JOHN C. NEWMAN

Making plans and securing a progressive future are more important now than ever before. The world is not in a thriving position. Tempers and temperatures are rising.

—JOHN C. NEWMAN

Humanity needs to grasp the fact that the future belongs to us all and will demand our involvement. Our attitudes toward individual involvement must change, or uncertainty and anarchy are in the future.

—JOHN C. NEWMAN

The future is happening now. The world is being threatened now. We must act now if we want to ensure a tranquil future.

—JOHN C. NEWMAN

Having to deal with constant chaos and conflict, combined with civil unrest, government, and humanity's polarization, is not by any means a healthy recipe for a prosperous future.

—JOHN C. NEWMAN

Society will not continue to tolerate the refusal to ensure equal justice for all or selectively enforcing laws and having separate consequences when crimes involve the elite, wealthy, and a select few. If not checked forthwith, insurrection is in the future.

—John C. Newman

There are so many who feel it is okay to do little and benefit from the efforts of the few. This mindset has become the norm rather than the exception. Step wide of these individuals; they are cancers and care not about the future's wellness.

—John C. Newman

We are all aware of the future; what it will bring is uncertain. However, humanity's actions will have dramatic implications for its outcome.

—John C. Newman

There is no crystal ball to ask about the future. Humanity has critical input. For the sake of having a progressive future, we must maintain our focus in the right direction.

—John C. Newman

The future is self-explanatory. What is going on in the world today is not beneficial or paints a promising picture of it.

—John C. Newman

Given the world's ever-increasing dilemmas, in the near future, humanity will be confronted with a daunting decision to make regarding its future wellbeing.

—JOHN C. NEWMAN

The future cannot be taken for granted. Our actions today have a major impact on tomorrow, which is synonymous with the future.

—JOHN C. NEWMAN

What the future will bring is always uncertain. Humanity's exploits at this point in time are frightening and not conducive to a prosperous one.

—JOHN C. NEWMAN

Society will always have a plethora of opportunities and a myriad of decisions to make. To secure a prosperous future, it is vital that the entire population's welfare is considered.

—JOHN C. NEWMAN

The future is on its way. It is crucial to what we do now. Society can ill afford to be cavalier.

—JOHN C. NEWMAN

It is unknown what the future will bring. The focus must be on today; the future handles itself.

—JOHN C. NEWMAN

Humanity must be careful of the decisions and choices being made, for there is a possibility that the future will reflect something unpleasant that has previously occurred. This would be a sad day.

—John C. Newman

The future is coming; nothing can be done to stop it. However, if we stop fighting among ourselves, this will have a positive influence.

—John C. Newman

For humanity to ensure a blissful future, we must concentrate on learning to depend on each other. It can give no regard to political affiliation, race, gender, creed, or color.

—John C. Newman

Our present and future are made up of many different facets. What society is doing now will have a major effect.

—John C. Newman

The future is what dreams are made of. Society must ensure that the future is something for all of us to look forward to.

—John C. Newman

World peace should be humanity's goal. If the people of the world would agree to commit to this course of action, what a fabulous future we would have!

—John C. Newman

A society unwilling to embrace and accept its past is destined for doom in the future.

—John C. Newman

If humanity's goal is to have a favorable future, it must demand that society make decisions that are in the best interest of all of its people.

—John C. Newman

When there is an erosion of society's ethics and a refusal to uphold laws designed to safeguard its people, these failures are definitely the makings for a bleak future.

—John C. Newman

What is essential is that society ensures our future is possible by making credible and informed decisions now.

—John C. Newman

The reason it is imperative that humanity focus on its future is because the future is dependent on what is being accomplished today.

—John C. Newman

No matter what humanity does, its future will not be known until it arrives. However, what it is presently doing is crucial.

—John C. Newman

The future concerns the world. Humanity must change its views of it forthwith and be cognizant of the fact that the actions being taken today will have a dramatic effect on the future.

—John C. Newman

Our future will be placed in jeopardy when society stops holding individuals accountable for their actions and enables irresponsible people.

—John C. Newman

Life's realism is that the future cannot be predicted or halted. Whatever it brings, what transpires will pass and be immutable. The future is history in the making.

—John C. Newman

For humanity to foster a prosperous and sustainable future, it must abandon idle promises and instead concentrate on tangible, positive corrective actions and accountability.

—John C. Newman

Our focus on the past should be brief; it will never return. However, we must remain vigilant because our future is hastily approaching.

—John C. Newman

9

DEFINING TRUE FRIENDSHIP

Upon reaching my golden years in life, I recall a multitude of wonderful Godsends, a few regrets, and fond memories of nurturing and sharing moments with many dear friends. In life, real friends are lifelong friends. They are true blessings we must cherish. It's crucial that we remember that the only way to have a true friend is to become one.

True friends are a living experience. They become more precious as time goes by. You will enjoy, disagree, grieve, share, argue, and have conflicts with each other, but that will never change your bond or devotion. In our life journey, these genuine individuals will always be there, lending their unwavering support and giving unconditional love.

—JOHN C. NEWMAN

Having true friends can be likened to being given a bouquet of beautiful flowers.

—JOHN C. NEWMAN

If we make one or two true friends in the course of life's journey, we can consider ourselves blessed.

—JOHN C. NEWMAN

Friendship can never be overrated. Unfortunately, however, it is sometimes taken advantage of.

—JOHN C. NEWMAN

If we are fortunate enough to have experienced the splendor of true friends in our lives, those endearing individuals will never be forgotten.

—JOHN C. NEWMAN

Throughout life, friendship can be unpredictable. At one juncture, we may be adversaries; at another, we have become the best of friends.

—JOHN C. NEWMAN

INTRODUCTION AND ACKNOWLEDGEMENTS

I am thankful for the presence of these carefully selected individuals in my life. They embody wisdom and the application of common sense. Their insightful words have also aided in guiding me throughout the process of writing "Thoughts of Wisdom: {The Simple Truths}."

Their names and quotes are listed arbitrarily:

Elders, Family, and Friends: R. Smith, A. Smith, M. Smith, H. Smith, R. Newman Sr., M. Newman, R. A. Ivy, L. Monroe, I. Davis, B. Bassie, M. Bassie, R. Newman, A. Newman, L. Newman, M. Bassie, O. Newman, M. Jenkins, S. Jenkins, B. Kimbrell, T. Williams, N. Williams, W. Bush, N. Bush, A. Gaines, H. Duvnjak. M. Duvnjak, D. Newman, J. Newman II, K. Lulic, O. White, a distinguished mature woman, a venerable senior gentleman, and unknown authors.

EDITOR

Journey with me: My primary objective is that your reading of "Thoughts of Wisdom {The Simple Truths}" makes you smile, touches your heart, and brings a playful harmony to your soul. I hope that somewhere in the text you witness a reflection of yourself while recalling fond memories of your loved one's family and friends. Moreover, I endeavored to keep my writing fresh and simplistic, for, in reality, life is simple and must be savored. We only have one life and a finite amount of time to live it. In truth, this book was written to share the blessings of my life journey.

Have you enjoyed this book?

We would love to hear from you!

Please send your comments to:
thoughtsofwisdomsimpletruths@gmail.com

Printed in the United States
by Baker & Taylor Publisher Services